Praise for *Seek the Peace of the City*

"Where this book helps me most are those chapters by Villafañe and his CUME colleagues on the enhancement and training of multiethnic leadership for the urban church."

— RAYMOND J. BAKKE
International Urban Associates

"Villafañe makes us participate in an uncomfortable dialogue where we can no longer escape behind traditional religiosity, stagnant pedagogy, or superficial social action. He reminds both the educational and the ecclesiastic institutions of the central role of the Holy Spirit in the on-going mission of the church, as well as the need to incarnate a truly good news of salvation for our cities. Must reading for all sincere Christians who seek an empowered ministry as they seek peace for our cities today."

— LOIDA MARTELL-OTERO
*Iglesia Bautista Cristiana de Soundview,
Bronx, New York*

"Villafañe presents a reason for why our evangelical engines must get on the move. As a Christian who has lived nearly all of his life in the city, he provides a wonderful integration of the social sciences with theology. His compassion and his passion for the gospel are evident; he moves from doing scholarly research to being an evangelist who is concerned with winning our cities for Jesus Christ."

— MANUEL ORTIZ
Westminster Theological Seminary

Seek the Peace of the City

Reflections on Urban Ministry

Eldin Villafañe

Foreword by
Harvey Cox

With chapters by
Douglas Hall
Efraín Agosto
Bruce W. Jackson

WILLIAM B. EERDMANS PUBLISHING COMPANY
GRAND RAPIDS, MICHIGAN

© 1995 Wm. B. Eerdmans Publishing Co.
255 Jefferson Ave. S.E., Grand Rapids, Michigan 49503
All rights reserved

Printed in the United States of America

00 99 98 97 96 95   7 6 5 4 3 2 1

Library of Congress Cataloging-in-Publication Data

Villafañe, Eldin, 1940-
Seek the peace of the city: reflections on urban ministry /
Eldin Villafañe; foreword by Harvey Cox; with chapters by
Douglas Hall, Efrain Agosto, Bruce W. Jackson.
        p.   cm.
Includes bibliographical references.
ISBN 0-8028-0729-1 (paper: alk. paper)
1. City churches. 2. City clergy. I. Hall, Douglas, 1937–
II. Agosto, Efrain.   III. Jackson, Bruce W.   IV. Title.
BV637.V55   1995
253'.09173'2 — dc20   95-20778
                                              CIP

Para
Margarita
("Margie")
Proverbios 31:10-31

Contents

Acknowledgments

The preparation of this book took place during my recovery from heart surgery. Margie and I wish to express our deepest appreciation and heartfelt thanks to my colleagues at Gordon-Conwell Theological Seminary, especially those at the Center for Urban Ministerial Education (CUME) in Boston, to many friends and churches across this country and abroad, and to our family. Your prayers and the many large and small acts of love and concern you shared were a profound source of joy and strength during this time.

I am grateful for the contributions made to this work by my friends and colleagues Douglas Hall, Efraín Agosto, and Bruce Jackson. Many years of ministry in metropolitan Boston, and valued time in play and prayer, have made our fellowship very dear to me.

Harvey Cox and I go back many years. I was privileged, during my doctoral studies days in the early 1970s, to take a course from him at Harvard. Our friendship began then and has developed over the years. Co-teaching several courses with him, both at Cambridge and in Roxbury, have made me value even more his great contribution to the church in our urban world. "Muchas gracias mi amigo" for your gracious words in the foreword.

Special thanks are in order for Naomi Wilshire. Naomi has been my faithful and competent secretary for about sixteen years — since she has been with CUME.

My prayer is that the Spirit of the living God will use this book to further challenge the people of God to "seek the peace of the city."

Credits

M ost of the chapters in this book have appeared in print in a variety of journals. Many chapters were also speeches delivered at different venues, all underscored by the context and challenges of the city. Some of the ideas and passages in this book appeared in an earlier form in my book *The Liberating Spirit*.

Introduction: "The Jeremiah Paradigm for the City," *Christianity and Crisis* (November 16, 1992): 374-75.

Chapter 1: "Scholarship as *Sierva, Santificadora,* and *Sanadora,*" *Apuntes* (Winter 1992): 147-49; presidential speech/paper at La Comunidad of Hispanic American Scholars of Theology and Religion, in conjunction with the Annual Meeting of the AAR/SBL, Kansas City, Missouri, November 25, 1991.

Chapter 2: "An Evangelical Call to a Social Spirituality: Confronting Evil in Urban Society," *Apuntes* (Summer 1991): 27-38; presented at Lausanne II in Manila, the International Congress on World Evangelization, Theology of the City, Urban Unit, Manila, the Philippines, July 11-20, 1989; and in a revised form at the Twentieth Annual Meeting of the Society for Pentecostal Studies (SPS), Dallas, Texas, November 8-10, 1990.

Chapter 3: "The Power of the Powerless: A Paradigm of Partnership from the Underside," speech presented at SCUPE, Congress on Urban Ministry, Chicago, Illinois, March 26, 1992.

Chapter 4: "Patience and the City," speech presented at CUME, tenth anniversary graduation celebration, Twelfth Baptist Church, Boston, May 1986.

Chapter 5: "An Approach to Winning Ethnic Minorities in the City," *New England Journal of Ministry* (Spring 1982): 54-60; presented at the fortieth Annual Convention of the National Association of Evangelicals (NAE), Chicago, Illinois, March 4, 1982.

Chapter 6: "Hispanic and African-American Racial Reconciliation: A 'Latin Jazz' Note," unpublished essay.

Chapter 7: "The Sociocultural Matrix of Intergenerational Dynamics: An Agenda for the 1990s," *Apuntes* (Spring 1992): 13-20; plenary speech at the Hispanic Association for Bilingual Bicultural Ministries (HABBM), New York City, June 1, 1991.

Chapter 8: "Essential Elements for an Effective Seminary-Based Urban Theological Education Program," paper commissioned by The PEW Charitable Trusts, Religion Program, 1991; read at the Academic Symposia, The Boston Theological Institute's 25th Year Anniversary Celebration, Harvard Divinity School, December 11, 1992; and included in Rodney L. Petersen, ed., *Christianity and Civil Society: Theological Education for Public Life* (Maryknoll, N.Y.: Orbis Books, 1995).

Chapter 9: Douglas Hall, "Theological Education in the Urban Context," in Ruy O. Costa, ed., *One Faith, Many Cultures: Inculturation, Indigenization, and Contextualization* (Maryknoll, N.Y.: Orbis Books; Boston: Boston Theological Institute, 1988), pp. 145-49.

Chapter 10: Efraín Agosto, "Paul, Leadership, and the Hispanic Church," *Urban Mission* (June 1993): 6-20.

Chapter 11: Bruce W. Jackson, "Urban Theological Education for Church Leadership," *Urban Mission* (December 1993): 32-43.

Foreword

The Christian faith came to birth in a world of teeming and conflict-ridden cities. Jesus himself began his ministry in Galilee, but he knew he would have to confront the corruption and tyranny of Jerusalem in order to complete his messianic mission. After the Resurrection and the descent of the Holy Spirit at Pentecost, tiny Christian congregations emerged in the great metropolitan areas of the Mediterranean world. In those heterogenous urban centers, Christians served the needs of the poor, and the gospel of life contended with the other living faiths of the day — the cults of Isis and Mithra, the decaying Roman pantheon, and the various Hellenistic philosophical schools.

Today, Christianity once again lives in a world of contending views of life and exploding cities. Indeed, the planet earth is quickly being transformed into what must appear from space to be a series of interactive megalopolises, whose suburbs and supportive surroundings reach out and mesh with each other. Television and computer networks bring urban culture into both the gleaming skyscraper and the rude hut. And the age of Christendom is over. Once again the Christian church is challenged by a variety of conflicting beliefs and philosophies, and by desperate human need.

This is the world in which all branches of the Christian church must now live and serve. This is particularly true of the evangelical wing of Christianity. In this book, Eldin Villafañe issues a ringing summons to all Christians, but to evangelical Christians in particular. In a winsome style that is informed both by a high degree of theological and social-scientific insight but also by a wealth of experience in the urban milieu, Villafañe lays out the vision of a church that does not retreat from the city but, in the spirit of the prophet Jeremiah, chooses to serve the urban community in the spirit of the gospel of Jesus Christ.

The summons this book issues is badly needed. Too many Christians today look upon the city, not as a place where God is moving to actualize signs of the coming kingdom, but as just so many Sodoms and Gomorrahs from which any decent person should beat a hasty retreat. Churches cautiously flee to the relative comfort of the suburbs and the exurbs, the so-called high potential areas for "church growth." But the high potential is often more for comfort and consumption than for prayer and witness, more for being at ease in Zion than for engaging both the destructive and the healing powers that the Spirit of God lets loose in the cities.

The Holy Spirit is central both to the mission of the church in today's urban world and to the vision of this book. Villafañe writes from his perspective as a Pentecostal theologian, a Puerto Rican pastor, a leader in the Hispanic community, and a pioneer of intercultural theological education. He demonstrates a lively style of social spirituality that does not require retreating to a cave or withdrawing to the green lawns of suburbia. He understands power and powerlessness, both as an astute sociologist and as a Christian believer who sees the power of the Spirit at work in unexpected places every day. He not only knows what it means to be part of a particular ethnic and linguistic minority today but he understands other minorities as well. He writes as a visionary who has already forged one of the most successful culturally diverse theological education programs in any city anywhere.

Villafañe's Pentecostal faith is central to his buoyant, but utterly realistic, hope for Christian ministry in the city. This should come as no surprise. The Pentecostal movement, the fastest-growing Christian grouping on the planet, now also finds itself at the crossroads of the great world city. Often mistakenly seen by critics and outsiders as the faith of backwoods believers, Pentecostalism actually first sprang to life in a culturally and racially mixed congregation in Los Angeles, spread to Chicago and New York and then across the seas, and is now growing fastest in the burgeoning cities of Asia, South America, and Africa.

But, like other Christian bodies, Pentecostals are frequently tempted to forget their urban origins and even their new urban frontiers and to look for what appear to be safer, cleaner, more homogeneous and less threatening places to minister. This book calls that temptation into sharp question. But it can do more than that. Like the Pentecostal movement itself, the underlying thrust of this volume has far more than a denominational significance. It is possible that the stunning growth of the Pentecostal movement signals an even larger change. It points to a "postmodern" world in which many people have not only grown tired of the rigidity and lack of experiential vitality in conventional religion but have also lost faith in the once bright promises of scientific modernity. Therefore, the appeal of those branches of Christianity that emphasize experience and participation are of enormous importance to all Christians and all people of faith. The Holy Spirit may be doing something much larger than even those who consciously testify to that Spirit's presence and power realize. I firmly believe that Pentecostalism, the tradition from which Villafañe writes, has something to say to all denominations of the Christian church as we all rethink our priorities and our mission in the high-speed, limbic, super-charged world culture that is breaking in upon us as the twentieth century breathes its last and the new millennium begins.

All this means that Villafañe's experience and insights, gathered carefully in this volume and presented with humor and clarity, should be required reading for anyone who seriously wants to know how to respond to the new things God is doing in our midst and to the new demands the Spirit places on our heads and our hearts.

HARVEY COX

▼ INTRODUCTION ▼

The Jeremiah Paradigm for the City

As a Puerto Rican Pentecostal, I have lived and ministered in the city almost all of my life. I have been called a "Pentecostal Liberationist." Some have thought that an oxymoron. But in reality the label makes sense when it is set within a theological understanding of the Holy Spirit as the Liberating Spirit.

Since the beginning of my ministry at "Iglesia Cristiana Juan 3:16" in the Bronx, over twenty-five years ago, I have been privileged to serve in many capacities in the urban scene. I was the founding director of the Center for Urban Ministerial Education of Gordon-Conwell Theological Seminary in Boston, a multilingual and multicultural urban theological center that serves over 300 students, representing 150 distinct churches, from 40 denominations and 22 nationalities. I served as director for fourteen years (1976–1990).

Through the years many books and persons have inspired and challenged my work in urban ministry. Yet, time and again, I have been driven by God's Spirit to find fresh inspiration in the words of the prophet Jeremiah: "And seek the Peace [Shalom] of the city . . . and pray to the Lord for it; for in its Peace [Shalom] you will have Peace [Shalom]" (29:7).

I am concerned for the city — particularly that inner-city reality that is being shaken by the mindless violence of its youth and undermined by the cold indifference of institutional violence. I am concerned with a church that has no mind for a wholistic vision for the city.

A very wise man of long ago, a man that knew a little of the

1

complexities of the city, said: "Where there is no vision, the people perish" (Prov. 29:18). The NIV reads as follows: "Where there is no revelation, the people cast off restraint." The absence of vision (or revelation) results in a "social meltdown," a moral and spiritual disintegration.

The prevalent "New Jack City" mentality of many urban youth, the unrestrained, rudderless, and destructive subculture so visible in our cities, is but a prophetic manifestation of a people perishing for lack of a *vision*. Individuals and institutions — including the church — that are to model and live out a vision are themselves visionless. A vision, whether we apply it to an individual or an institution, gives direction, focuses energies, informs content and character, and sets the framework for "seeing" and "valuing" life's true meaning and goals. It shapes the image of self and world.

Jeremiah's words are instructive here. They present a new challenge to God's people in a new reality. They address the question: What is the role of the people of God in the city? Or, to bring it closer to home: What is the role of the church (God's people) in the city today? Jeremiah's answer — I call it "The Jeremiah Paradigm for the City" — is an overarching, wholistic vision for the city, one that can inspire our work in urban ministry in the 1990s.

PRESENCE, PEACE, PRAYER

Jeremiah's paradigm stems from a theology of context,.a theology of mission, and a theology of spirituality. Corresponding to it are three key words: presence, peace, and prayer.

Presence: Jeremiah 29:5-6 speaks to me, to the church, of our relationship to the city, to culture and society. Jeremiah's words to those exiled in Babylon are still relevant. Against the false prophets who might call for "assimilation," "revolution," or "escapism," Jeremiah called for "critical engagement" — for presence!

I am helped by the etymology of the word *church (ekklesia)*. In ancient Greece it referred to the congregation or assembly of the "called out ones" to discuss the situation of the *polis* — the city! The church gathers to worship and to equip itself to impact the polis. It does not live for itself, but for the kingdom (rule, sovereignty) of God. The church cannot be indifferent to the human needs in the city — be they physical, political, economic, or spiritual. It does not hide, neither does it integrate falsely in society. But it is present as salt and light in all the affairs of the polis.

Peace: Jeremiah 29:7*a* speaks to me, to the church, of our mission in the city. The word *peace* (Shalom) best summarizes that mission. Martin Luther King, Jr., understood this well when he stated that "true peace is not merely the absence of tension, it is the presence of justice." Shalom speaks of wholeness, soundness, completeness, health, harmony, reconciliation, justice, welfare — both personal and social. The church is an instrument, a servant, of peace in the city. It preaches and lives out the Shalom of God.

I need to be reminded, the church needs to be reminded, with Peter in the house of Cornelius (Acts 10:36): "You know the message God sent . . . telling the *good news of peace* through Jesus Christ, who is Lord of all."

Prayer: Jeremiah 29:7*b* speaks to me, to the church, of the spirituality needed to struggle and live in the city. A true urban spirituality knows the critical importance of prayer; it knows that the struggle requires the nurturing and "caring of the soul." Spiritual power encounters are indeed present in the polis. Equipped with the whole armor of God, we go out to confront the principalities and powers.

▼ PART ONE ▼

URBAN SOCIO-THEOLOGY

CHAPTER 1

Scholarship as *Sierva,*
Santificadora, and *Sanadora*

The emergence in the middle and late 1980s of ACHTUS (Academy of Catholic Hispanic Theologians of the United States) and La Comunidad of Hispanic American Scholars of Theology and Religion is an occasion for celebration. We celebrate the "coming of age" and the "coming together" of scholars from diverse disciplines and religious traditions of our one Christian faith and Hispanic heritage.

La Comunidad, whose first objective is "to promote and stimulate scholarship for and by Hispanic American scholars," is on its way in making significant contributions in the broad fields of theological and religious studies. The academic credentials and commitment to serious reflection by our members is commendable. Yet, at this early stage of La Comunidad's development it is critical for us to reflect on "with whom" and "for whom" is this scholarship. I will use three metaphors *(Sierva, Santificadora,* and *Sanadora)* to share with you my deep concern — a pastoral concern, if you will — for the *Quo Vadis* of our scholarship. As you will note, this is both a preliminary and a sketchy attempt to preempt a trajectory that has been the *maldición y muerte* of traditional scholarship in the guild.

SCHOLARSHIP AS *SIERVA*

Our self-understanding (identity) as Christians precludes any other understanding of calling (vocation) than that of servants. Whether we are laypersons or ministers, professors or students, whatever our human vocation and wherever we exercise our gifts, we are called to service.

In the person and work of our Lord Jesus Christ the paradigm par excellence has been set. Jesus' missional self-understanding (Luke 4:18-19; Mark 10:45) also informs our missional self-understanding as scholars. "For even the Son of Man did not come to be served, but to serve, and to give his life as a ransom for many" (Mark 10:45, NIV). Our being scholars, more and not less, demands that we reappropriate Jesus' missional self-understanding "to preach the gospel to the poor . . . to heal the brokenhearted, to preach deliverance to the captives" (Luke 4:18). Scholarship fulfills Jesus' missional self-understanding, and thus its true calling, when it is committed to be a *Sierva* of the poor and oppressed. Scholarship is not defined, nor does it fulfill its *razón de ser,* by a self-serving exercise of pure *pedantería.*

Scholarship as *Sierva* places its academic gifts and resources before the Hispanic church and community in the service of interpreting and responding to its needs and vision. Scholarship as *Sierva* is a posture, process, and project of good news for our Hispanic church and community. While an authentic scholarship will also serve the broader universe of discourse in academia and other circles in our society, we must be clear that the academic guild — or for that matter truth with a small "t" — is not our "reference point." Scholarship as *Sierva* no longer follows the "pied piper" of the elite, white (and male) intellectual/academic establishment's agenda. But make no mistake, scholarship as *Sierva* demands more, not less, academic rigor, analytical and synthetic powers, and intellectual integrity.

Scholarship as *Sierva* sets before itself an agenda informed by the struggles and joys of our Hispanic church and community. Scholarship as *Sierva* knows with whom it is in solidarity. It too seeks to be a liberating agent of the Spirit as God's reign breaks in and among us. In an extension of the metaphor, scholarship as *María la Sierva* is pregnant with possibilities for and with "them of low degree" (Luke 1:52).

SCHOLARSHIP AS SANTIFICADORA

Scholarship as *Santificadora* speaks of our prophetic task. It calls for an understanding of sanctification as separation and denunciation of all *pecado y mal*. Scholarship as *Santificadora* means that our scholarly production, published or manifested in our teaching, challenges *el pecado y el mal* that shows itself in persons and institutions. It is not neutral nor value free in the ongoing struggle waged against God's reign by the "principalities and powers." Our scholarship should be more clear and intentional in terms of whose benefit is accrued by its production. For after all is said and done, scholarly production is a political act. As such, scholarship as *Santificadora* blows the cover off the myth of nonpolitical or apolitical scholarship.

Scholarship as *Santificadora* serves as a voice for the voiceless. In our *barrios* there are sisters and brothers who need a voice, a scholarly voice, to speak with and for them as they respond to the *miseria* and *basura* around them. With drugs, crime, AIDS, drop-outs, and poverty rampant in our *barrios,* I often ask myself, where are our scholars? Our youth, as well as our elders, need all the scholarly resources that we can place at their disposal to denounce *el pecado y el mal*. Our respective academic disciplines, be they biblical studies, theology, ethics, history, Christian education, or any of the other ministerial fields, can play a vital prophetic task in the *barrios*.

Scholarship as *Santificadora* will speak to the church and the community as well as to the "powers that be." Scholarship as *Santificadora* will, thus, challenge the church to be the church. It will call the church not to be simply a "worldly" and "successful" institution preoccupied with its own maintenance and survival, but to be a true sign of the reign of God: a "free space" where the liberating grace of our Lord Jesus Christ sets people free to and for God, for each other, and for the world. Scholarship as *Santificadora* will challenge the "powers that be" by calling for repentance and restitution — by calling for justice.

SCHOLARSHIP AS SANADORA

Scholarship as *Sanadora* speaks of a community of scholars who by presence and production (by being and doing) contribute to the healing, to the Shalom, of our Hispanic church and community.

I am deeply concerned that our academic training and often the locus of our academic service disengages us from our *Pueblo*. Scholarship as *Sanadora* requires that we be *presentes* with our *Pueblo*. Some of us have paid a price in being "too much" of a presence, perhaps to the detriment of quantitative scholarly production. Yet, one hopes that this presence with our *Pueblo* will result in qualitative scholarly output.

In our Hispanic churches there are many "ills" that need our scholarly attention. Let me highlight just one of these ills. The socioeconomic context and the cultural ethos of contemporary society have produced in many of our churches an obsession with simply quantitative growth. Do not get me wrong, I believe in numerical growth, yet an inordinate focus on this area of church growth can result in an unhealthy church. A healthy growing church must grow in all the classical missional dimensions. It must demonstrate by word and deed a true *Kerygma, Koinonia, Diakonia,* and *Leitourgia.*

A healthy church's proclamation of the good news comes to terms with a holistic understanding of the gospel's role in personal and social transformation. Its good news is the good news of the inbreaking of the reign of God. A healthy church must model for a broken world a true fellowship or community of the Spirit; a "free space" where forgiveness is experienced and offered to all. A healthy church is a church of the *toalla y palangana,* serving the needy in and among them. A healthy church is ultimately by posture and program a worshiping congregation. It is a church that is constantly reminded that we worship one living God and not the many "idols" of our consumer society.

Scholarship as *Sanadora* is being an intellectual nurse or physician serving the ills and wounds in our church and *barrios.* It is bringing to bear all the expertise of our respective disciplines to ask and attempt to answer the question: "How can I help to heal a church, a community, a society wounded by racism, sexism, classism; wounded by hate, arrogance, and power; and wounded by all manner of oppression and sin?"

We have a great challenge before us as Hispanic scholars in La Comunidad. The best years are before us. Will we be seduced by the guild and the academic establishment to bow before their agenda? Or will we reappropriate our missional agenda from the Lord Jesus Christ and redefine and commit ourselves to a paradigm that sees scholarship as *Sierva, Santificadora,* and *Sanadora?*

CHAPTER 2

An Evangelical Call to a Social Spirituality: Confronting Evil in Urban Society

As we enter the twenty-first century, there is no greater need for evangelicals in the cities than to articulate, in both word and deed, a social spirituality. The twin phenomena of urbanization and globalization, which define the ethos of our great cities, demand no more and no less than an authentically biblical spirituality. If the whole church is to take the whole gospel to the whole world, it must have a "wholistic" spirituality.

A spirituality, if it is to be authentic and relevant, should correlate with all of life; for after all the Spirit of the Lord, who leads and empowers, must lead and empower all areas of our life. Spirituality has been defined as "a particular style of approach to union with God,"[1] "a following of Jesus,"[2] "a style of living the life of the Holy Spirit,"[3] or my own personal definition, which synthesizes a trinitarian and moral thrust, "in obedience to God, the following of Jesus in the power of the

1. George A. Lane, *Christian Spirituality: An Historical Sketch* (Chicago: Loyola Univ. Press, 1984), p. 2.

2. Gustavo Gutiérrez, *We Drink from Our Own Wells: The Spiritual Journey of a People* (Maryknoll, N.Y.: Orbis, 1984), p. 1.

3. Frances X. Meehan, *A Contemporary Social Spirituality* (Maryknoll, N.Y.: Orbis, 1982), p. 1.

Spirit." Undergirding these various definitions is a self-understanding of a loving heart yearning, seeking, and responding as a whole person, in the obedience of faith, to a loving God.

The history of the spiritualities of the church reflects the spiritual pilgrimage of particular individuals and particular people at a particular time and in a particular context. The times we live in, the cities we live in, and the gospel we live by call us to a spirituality that goes beyond, though yet includes, "a personal transfiguration into the image of Christ."[4]

One can surely make a case for the emergence at distinct periods throughout the church (both Catholic and Protestant) of what can be termed a wholistic spirituality — covering "the following of Jesus" in both personal transformation/piety and social transformation/piety. Yet by and large our contemporary evangelical spirituality has been defined by only the individualistic and personal dimension. This personal transformation into the image of Christ, by grace, through faith, by means of the Word, prayer, contemplation, and the exercise of the "spiritual disciplines," is thus inner-directed and vertical. The missing dimension of social transformation/piety (which includes social witness, social service, and social action, and is thus outer-directed and horizontal) as "bona fide" spirituality has often been excluded from an authentically biblical and evangelical definition of spirituality. The call is to redefine and reappropriate from Scripture and from the rich heritage of the church a social spirituality that is consistent with the "following of Jesus."

Jesus Christ, the Anointed One (Luke 4:18; Acts 10:38), is the paradigm *par excellence* of this spirituality. Through the power of the Spirit the believer is both "being transformed into his likeness with ever-increasing glory, which comes from the Lord, who is the Spirit" (2 Cor. 3:18) and challenged to follow him: "as the Father has sent me, I am sending you . . . receive the Holy Spirit" (John 20:21-22). Thus, the double focus and goal of Christian spirituality has (1) a vertical focus — the continual transformation into the likeness of Jesus, the resurrected Lord; and (2) a horizontal focus — the following of Jesus, in similar obedience of the Father's missional calling (Luke 4:18-19).

4. Donald G. Bloesch, *The Struggle of Prayer* (Colorado Springs, Col.: Helmers & Howard, 1988), p. 3.

Both of these foci and goals can only be carried out in the power of the Spirit, and undergirded by God's love. Both have a vertical and horizontal dimension that interrelates them and dynamically "nourishes" them. "Transformation" needs "following" and "following" needs "transformation." Both have a personal and social dimension that equally interrelates them and dynamically "nourishes" them.

The "vertical-transformation" focus and its interrelationship with the horizontal are noted well in 1 John 4:7-13 (NIV):

> . . . let us love one another, for love comes from God. Everyone who loves has been born of God and knows God. Whoever does not love does not know God, because God is love. This is how God showed his love among us: He sent his one and only Son into the world that we might live through him. This is love: not that we loved God, but that he loved us and sent his Son as an atoning sacrifice for our sins. . . . Since God so loved us, we also ought to love one another. No one has ever seen God; but *if we love one another, God lives in us and his love is made complete in us.* We know that *we live in him* and *he in us,* because he has given us of *his Spirit.*

The "horizontal-following" focus and its interrelationship with the vertical are noted well by Jesus' missional self-understanding (which should also be ours) in Luke 4:18-19 (NIV):

> The *Spirit of the Lord is on me,* because he has *anointed me* to preach good news to the poor. He has sent me to proclaim freedom for the prisoners and recovery of sight for the blind, to release the oppressed, to proclaim the year of the Lord's favor.

This dynamic and dialectical spirituality is to be "worked out" in a social context — a social context that deeply needs both contemplative and apostolic activity. The brokenness of society (so visible in the *barrios* and ghettos of our cities), the scriptural missional mandate, and the Spirit's love constrain us to feed the hungry, visit the sick and prisoners, shelter the homeless and poor — to express God's love in social concerns. We do this as an expression of faithful obedience and authentic spirituality.

In the latter part of this century, through the careful reading and rereading of Scripture (especially from the context of the "periphery") and the critical utilization of the analytical tools of the social sciences, we have gained a new understanding of our social reality. The concomitant Pentecostal/charismatic outpouring of the Spirit, also in this century, has brought to many a critical awareness and discernment of the depth and complexity of sin — the "mystery of iniquity."

There is a need to extend the evangelicals' classical understanding of spirituality's struggles with the flesh, the world, and the devil with their social correlates, namely, sinful social structures, the "world" *(kosmos)*, and "principalities and powers." The evangelical church is thus challenged to acknowledge that an authentic and relevant spirituality must be wholistic, responding to both the vertical and horizontal dimension of life. The inclusion of the social dimension in a redefinition of spirituality is the missing ingredient of contemporary evangelical spirituality.

Let me move now to consider elements contributing to a social spirituality. These elements will be presented under four major headings: (1) The Spirit's "Grieving" — Sin: Personal and Social; (2) Mystery of Iniquity: The Texture of Social Existence; (3) The Gospel of the Reign of God; and (4) The Challenge to Confront Structural Sin and Evil.

THE SPIRIT'S "GRIEVING" — SIN: PERSONAL AND SOCIAL[5]

The spiritual pilgrimage of the believer is a pilgrimage of love. Any true spirituality is ultimately the loving of God and neighbor as oneself (Matt. 19:19) — the integration of the spiritual and the ethical, of worship and service, and of identity and vocation. Love is often easier to acknowledge than to define. What Augustine said of time can probably be said of love: "If no one asks me, I know, if I wish to explain it to one that asketh, I know not."[6] In any description love is deeply personal. The love of God in Christ poured out by the Holy Spirit establishes a

5. See Eph. 4:30; 5:1-2 (NIV).
6. Augustine, *Confessions*, bk. 2 (New York: Random House, n.d.), p. 253, quoted in Meehan, *Contemporary Social Spirituality*, p. 1.

loving relationship with God that — as with all love affairs, particularly the human response — is subject to the vacillations, voids, and vicissitudes of life.

As mere humans in a spiritual pilgrimage of love, we grieve the object of our love often. Whether the grieving of that object of love be human or divine (in our immediate understanding of the object), it is ultimately a grieving of the Spirit. The "love of the Spirit" (Rom. 15:30) can be grieved.

A careful exegesis of Paul's admonition in Ephesians 4:5 places the context of the grieving of the Spirit within an ethico-spiritual relationship with others. These attitudes and actions of the believers that "cut" the relationship of love and thus grieve the Holy Spirit are called sin in Scripture. In the biblical revelation sin can be more broadly described as *disobedience* to the Lordship of God, *injustice* and alienation, and *unbelief* and idolatry.[7] We sin, thus the Spirit is grieved, when we do not imitate God, sacrificially give up ourselves as Christ did, and "live a life of love" (Eph. 4:30; 5:1-2).

The apostle Paul clearly teaches that sin is a harsh taskmaster, "for the wages of sin is death" (Rom. 6:23a). The predicament of *all* persons is death — separation from God, from others, from themselves, and even from creation. Scripture is quite clear that individual action has marked social implications. It likewise notes that social or corporate action has marked individual implications.[8] Sin, while being deeply personal, is not just individualistic. The person as a *socius* ("person-in-community") is vividly portrayed by Paul's anthropological understanding of "corporate personality" as noted in Romans 5:12: "just as sin entered the world through one man, and death through sin, and in this way death came to all men, because all sinned." Orlando Costas notes, commenting on this verse, that

---

7. See Orlando Costas, *Christ Outside the Gate: Mission Beyond Christendom* (Maryknoll, N.Y.: Orbis, 1982), pp. 21-24; see also Walter Grundmann, *hamartano*, *Theological Dictionary of the New Testament*, vol. 1, ed. Gerhard Kittel, trans. Geoffrey W. Bromiley (Grand Rapids: Eerdmans, 1964), pp. 267-316.

8. In Scripture there are many cases (i.e., Joshua 7; Rom. 5:12-21) that illustrate this truth of the interrelatedness of human personality in the web of other persons and actions. For the Hebrew conception of this "corporate personality" see H. Wheeler Robinson, *Corporate Personality in Ancient Israel* (Philadelphia: Fortress, 1964).

The sin of one man affected all, because "all" were represented already in the one. Therefore guilt and condemnation have passed to all. All are guilty of sin, not just because they personally sin, but because they are part of Adam. Thus sin is both personal and social.[9]

Sin and its work are a reality in all human experience. No area of personal and human history is left untouched by its destructive reality. It is ultimately and radically death/separation from God.

The response to sin and death is the need for the loving initiative of the Spirit of God to convict of sin, righteousness, and judgment (John 16:8-11), based on the equally radical answer of "the crucified God."[10] Paul speaks eloquently of the multifaceted drama of redemption that deals with sin and death:

> But God, who is rich in mercy, for his great love wherewith he loved us, even when we were dead in sins, hath quickened us together with Christ (by grace ye are saved), and hath raised us up together, and made us sit together in heavenly places in Christ Jesus. (Eph. 2:4-6, KJV)

The power of sin and death is broken. In the cross of Christ the believer has the resources to overcome its dominion. My colleague, David F. Wells, notes that "the world, the flesh, and the devil are not invincible competitors but doomed adversaries. In the work on the Cross, Christ conquered them, and through the work of the Spirit, that conquest is brought into our modern world."[11]

It grieves the Spirit when believers manifest the works of sin. Paul in his letter to the Galatians (chap. five) notes that sin's work in human nature (*sarx*, "the flesh")[12] is the antithesis of the Spirit's fruit. The

9. Costas, *Christ Outside the Gate*, p. 25. Both Paul and Costas implicitly underline in this passage not just the universality of sin but equally its manifestation in corporate personality.

10. See Jürgen Moltmann, *The Crucified God: The Cross of Christ as the Foundation and Criticism of Christian Theology* (New York: Harper and Row, 1974).

11. David F. Wells, *God the Evangelist: How the Holy Spirit Works to Bring Men and Women to Faith* (Grand Rapids: Eerdmans, 1987), p. 67.

12. Richard Lovelace's words are instructive:

> The New Testament designates the total organism of sin by the term *sarx* (flesh), referring to the fallen human personality apart from the renewing influence and

Spirit's fruit (love, joy, peace, patience, kindness, goodness, faithfulness, gentleness, and self-control; Gal. 5:22-23) is the believer-lover's attestation of growth in his or her spirituality. The Spirit's fruit are both sign and substance of "transformation" to Christ's image, and moral virtues needed in the following of him. They are marks of genuine spirituality. The Spirit seeks to restore the fellowship broken by sin and to overcome the separation in a bond of love.

MYSTERY OF INIQUITY:
THE TEXTURE OF SOCIAL EXISTENCE[13]

Article 12 of the Lausanne Covenant notes that the church is engaged in spiritual warfare with principalities and powers of evil. It is within the framework of the ongoing cosmic conflict between God and Satan, and the restraining power of the Holy Spirit, that any discussion of sin — particularly in its powerful and mysterious (secret) structural or institutional manifestations — must be set.

Social Reality

From the social sciences, particularly the sociology of knowledge, we have learned that the institutions and structures of social life are more than the sum of the individuals that make it up.[14] Society is a dialectic

---

control of the Holy Spirit. The flesh is always somewhat mysterious to us, particularly in its effect on our minds and its operation in the redeemed personality. The New Testament constantly describes it as something much deeper than the isolated moments of sin which it generates. (*Dynamics of Spiritual Life* [Downers Grove, Ill.: InterVarsity Press, 1979], pp. 89-90)

13. See 2 Thess. 2:7. "Our struggle with evil must correspond to the geography of evil." Stephen Charles Mott, *Biblical Ethics and Social Change* (New York: Oxford Univ. Press, 1982), p. 16.

14. See esp. Peter L. Berger and Thomas Luckman, *The Social Construction of Reality: A Treatise in the Sociology of Knowledge* (New York: Anchor Books, 1967); Peter L. Berger, *The Sacred Canopy: Elements of a Sociological Theory of Religion* (New York: Anchor Books, 1969).

phenomenon that is a human product, as well as a producer of the human. Social institutions are basically routinized human patterned norms and behaviors for social living (i.e., family, schools, laws, religion, political and social systems). Some institutions (i.e., family, work, the state) may even be categorized as a "given," as God's "orders of creation," "divine orders," or "structures of creation."[15] Thus, they are seen as God's gracious gifts to human beings for social existence and in which, as Emil Brunner reminds us, "even if only in a fragmentary and indirect way, God's will meets us."[16]

All social structures and institutions "have moral values embedded in them. They can be good or evil."[17] To speak of sinful structures and institutions is to speak of structures and institutions that have become distorted, misguided, destructive, or oppressive.[18] As such they are in need of liberation — by dismantling, reconstruction, transformation, revolution, or "exorcism" — by human and divine power. What is significant to note is that the texture of social existence reveals the presence of institutions and structures that regulate life, that seem to have an objective reality independent of the individual, and thus can become oppressive, sinful, or evil. We are all part of this texture of social existence, and our spiritual living is impacted by this complex web.[19]

Principialities and Powers

The "powers," as they are often noted in current biblical, theological, and ethical discussions,[20] speak to us that beyond personal sin and evil,

---

15. See esp. Emil Brunner, *The Divine Imperative* (Philadelphia: Westminster, 1937), and Pedro Arana Quiroz, "Ordenes de la Creación y Responsabilidad Cristiana," in *Fe Cristiana y Latinoamérica Hoy,* ed. C. René Padilla (Buenos Aires: Ediciones Certeza, 1974), pp. 169-84.

16. Brunner, *Divine Imperative,* p. 291.

17. Meehan, *Contemporary Social Spirituality,* p. 9.

18. See Patrick Kerans, *Sinful Social Structures* (New York: Paulist, 1974).

19. For an early and provocative treatment that deals with sinful and evil social structures, see Walter Rauschenbusch's chapters, "The Super-personal Forces of Evil" and "The Kingdom of Evil," in his *A Theology for the Social Gospel* (New York: Macmillan, 1917), pp. 69-94.

20. See, among others, Hendrikus Berkhof, *Christ and the Powers* (Scottdale, Pa.:

beyond social structures embedded with sinful or evil moral designs, beyond sinful and evil systems of values, there exists evil "in the social and political roles of powerful supernatural beings."[21] The texture of social existence is indeed permeated by "the mystery of iniquity." Yet, we must note with my colleague, Stephen C. Mott, that "these biblical concepts relate to phenomena which can be sociologically described and they extend rather than nullify personal responsibility in society."[22]

Contra Berkhof and others, Mott posits that these "principalities and powers" are angelic powers, not depersonalized social forces or principles. His careful exegesis of Scripture and pertinent Hellenistic and Jewish apocalyptic literature compels him to "stress this background, not to bring the occult into the understanding of institutional evil, but because it shows the political and social significance of the powers."[23]

Our struggle for an authentic and social spirituality must be cognizant that "our struggle is not against flesh and blood, but against the rulers *[archai]*, against the authorities *[exousiai]*, against the powers of this dark world *[kosmokratores]*" (Eph. 6:12). These are "powers" who rebelled against God, and, as John H. Yoder reminds us, "were part of the good creation of God."[24] Their original power and authority over creation included its social and political life. This authority given by God for providential care has resulted in oppression. They are fallen "powers" with idolatrous-demonic claims. Notwithstanding their fallen condition they "cannot fully escape the providential sovereignty of God. He is still able to use them for good."[25] Yoder categorizes the "powers" as religious structures, intellectual structures (-ologies and -isms), moral

---

Herald, 1962); Jacques Ellul, *The Subversion of Christianity* (Grand Rapids: Eerdmans, 1987), pp. 174-90; Mott, *Biblical Ethics,* pp. 3-21; Jim Wallis, *Agenda for Biblical People* (New York: Harper and Row, 1976), pp. 38-55; Walter Wink, *Naming the Powers: The Language of Powers in the New Testament* (Philadelphia: Fortress, 1984); Wink, *Unmasking the Powers: The Invisible Forces that Determine Human Existence* (Philadelphia: Fortress, 1986); John H. Yoder, *The Politics of Jesus* (Grand Rapids: Eerdmans, 1972), pp. 135-62.

21. Mott, *Biblical Ethics,* p. 6.
22. Ibid., p. 4.
23. Ibid., p. 8.
24. Yoder, *Politics of Jesus,* p. 143.
25. Ibid., p. 144.

structures (codes and customs), political structures (the tyrant, the market, the school, the court, race, and nation).[26] The ambivalent status of humanity relative to the "powers" and their manifestations in structures, institutions, and other corporate realities are noted by Yoder under two statements: "we cannot live without them . . . we cannot live with them."[27] Yoder states that

> There could not be society or history, there could not be man without the existence above him of religious, intellectual, moral and social structures. *We cannot live without them.* These structures are not and never have been a mere sum total of the individuals composing them. The whole is more than the sum of its parts. And this "more" is an invisible Power, even though we may not be used to speaking of it in personal or angelic terms.
>
> But these structures fail to serve man as they should. They do not enable him to live a genuinely free, human, loving life. They have absolutized themselves and they demand from the individual and society an unconditional loyalty. They harm and enslave man. *We cannot live with them.*[28]

What is most significant to note at this time is that the "powers" have been defeated and carried captive by Christ. "And having disarmed the powers and authorities, he made a public spectacle of them, triumphing over them by the cross" (Col. 2:15, NIV). The "powers" have been "disarmed" by Christ; we need not absolutize or respond to their idolatrous-demonic claims. This "good news" is part and parcel of our demonstration and proclamation of the gospel of Jesus Christ.

In concluding this section, it is important to note that

> the existence of an evil order ruled by supernatural beings must either be accepted or rejected on faith, but such reality would not be dis-

---

26. Ibid., p. 145.

27. Ibid., p. 146.

28. Ibid., pp. 145-46 (italics his). It is interesting to note that Yoder thinks that traditional theologies have sought to describe and treat this theme under the "orders of creation." He finds them wanting, though, in that they were not able to affirm "that it is in Christ that these values all find their meaning and coherence" (ibid., pp. 146-47).

sonant with our social experience. Our concern here is not to settle the cosmological question of whether angels and demons should be demythologized but rather to come to terms with social material to which their biblical existence points. . . . The world-order and the evil presence of the powers are never *synonymous* with the concrete forms of social and institutional life. Institutions function both to enslave and to liberate human existence. The powers are always present along with enslavement and death in small or large degree; but their real existence is behind the scenes in a system of hostile values vying for control of the life of the world.[29]

Any and every spirituality to be authentic and relevant must come to terms with personal and social sin and evil. What is most critical for an evangelical spirituality is to incorporate within its theology and ethics, not to say its spirituality, a "deeper" understanding of the "mystery of iniquity." It must realize that sin and evil go beyond the individual; that we are all enmeshed in a social living that is complex, dynamic, and dialectical; and that our spirituality, and the very gospel that we preach, needs to be as big and ubiquitous as sin and evil.[30] We will falter in our spirituality and thus grieve the Spirit if "our struggle with evil" does not "correspond to the geography of evil." We are assured in this struggle that

> we are more than conquerors through him who loved us. For I am convinced that neither death nor life, neither angels nor demons, neither the present nor the future, nor any powers, neither height nor depth, nor anything else in all creation, will be able to separate us from the love of God that is in Christ Jesus our Lord. (Rom. 8:37-39, NIV)

29. Mott, *Biblical Ethics,* pp. 10, 15 (italics his).

30. For a provocative and insightful study that integrates theology with the findings of clinical psychology in interpreting certain "non-physical realities," see Morton Kelsey, *Discernment: A Study in Ecstasy and Evil* (New York: Paulist, 1978).

GOSPEL OF THE REIGN OF GOD[31]

Eschatology forms the central and essential framework of New Testament theology. The "beginning" of the End, the reign of God, has broken into our world in the person of Jesus. The message of the New Testament is that God's royal rule is *already* present in Jesus the Messiah, although it awaits final consummation in the *not yet* of the future. In Jesus Christ we have, in the words of George Eldon Ladd, the "fulfillment without consummation" of the reign of God.[32]

The "good news" of the reign meant that beyond God's governing through creation and providence his special reign or rule had broken into history. It is important to note that "the Greek word *basileia,* which is used for *reign* or *kingdom,* means primarily the *act* of reigning rather than the *place* of reigning; thus in most cases it should be translated as *reign, rule, kingship* or *sovereignty,* rather than its usual English rendering, *kingdom.*"[33]

Jesus himself both proclaimed and embodied the reign. John Wimber notes,

> This explains the two-fold pattern of Christ's ministry, repeated wherever he went: first *proclamation,* then *demonstration.* First he preached repentance and the good news of the Kingdom of God. Then he cast out demons, healed the sick, raised the dead — which proved he was the presence of the Kingdom, the Anointed One.[34]

31. See Matt. 12:28.

32. George Eldon Ladd, *The Presence of the Future: The Eschatology of Biblical Realism* (Grand Rapids: Eerdmans, 1974), pp. 105-21. Among the many other pertinent works on the reign of God, see Ladd, *A Theology of the New Testament* (Grand Rapids: Eerdmans, 1983); Karl Ludwig Schmidt, *Basileus — Basilikos, TDNT,* 1:564-93; John Bright, *The Kingdom of God* (Nashville: Abingdon, 1953); Herman Ridderbos, *The Coming of the Kingdom* (Philadelphia: Presbyterian and Reformed, 1962); Amos N. Wilder, "Kerygma, Eschatology and Social Ethics," in *The Background of the New Testament and Its Eschatology,* ed. W. D. Davies and D. Daube (Cambridge: Cambridge Univ. Press, 1956), pp. 509-36; C. René Padilla, *Mision Integral: Ensayos Sobre el Reino y la Iglesia* (Grand Rapids: Eerdmans, 1986).

33. In Mott, *Biblical Ethics,* pp. 82-83 (italics his).

34. John Wimber, *Power Evangelism* (San Francisco: Harper and Row, 1986), p. 6.

The reign of God in Jesus is one of "spiritual power encounters."[35] Jesus' life and mission were both inaugurated and empowered by the Holy Spirit. David Wells states, "so it is that Jesus' birth, baptism, miracles, teaching, sacrifice, and resurrection are all ascribed to the working of the Holy Spirit."[36] Roger Stronstad can thus speak of Jesus' life and mission as that of the charismatic Christ. He goes on to state that "Jesus is not only anointed by the Spirit, but He is also Spirit-led, Spirit-filled, and Spirit-empowered."[37] Jesus' mission is one of the Spirit's anointment for "spiritual power encounters."[38]

The powers of the age to come have indeed invaded this age. The "signs and wonders" were and still are a witness to this reality. The reign of God has come because the "strong man's house" has been invaded by the charismatic Christ (Matt. 12:28). C. René Padilla states that

> the kingdom of darkness that pertains to this age has been invaded; the "strong man" has been disarmed, conquered, and robbed (Mt. 12:29; Lk. 11:22). . . . In other words, the historic mission of Jesus can only be understood in connection with the Kingdom of God. His mission here and now is the manifestation of the Kingdom as a present reality in his own person and action, in his preaching of the Gospel and in his works of justice and mercy.[39]

The gospel of the reign of God is the good news that in the life, death, and resurrection of Christ, God's reign is manifested in the physical and historical affairs of people — bound and hindered by demonic forces — now able to experience the Spirit's total liberation.[40] God's salvation in Christ affects the whole person — both spiritual and physical — in his or her concrete historical reality. Nothing is exempt from

---

35. See, among others, Wimber, ibid.; Roger Stronstad, *The Charismatic Theology of St. Luke* (Peabody, Mass.: Hendrickson, 1984); and David F. Wells, "Spiritual Power Encounters" in Wells, *God the Evangelist*, pp. 65-91.

36. Wells, *God the Evangelist*, p. 29.

37. Stronstad, *Charismatic Theology*, p. 45.

38. "The Spirit of the Lord is on me, because he has anointed me to preach good news to the poor. He has sent me to proclaim freedom for the prisoners and recovery of sight for the blind, to release the oppressed, to proclaim the year of the Lord's favor" (Luke 4:18-19, NIV).

39. Padilla, *Mision Integral*, p. 182.

40. Mott, *Biblical Ethics*, p. 94.

God's reign. While we live in the *not yet* of complete fulfillment of the reign of God that awaits the *parousia* in the future, we nevertheless continue to share in Jesus' mission of liberation through *proclamation* and *demonstration* (see John 20:21).

The early church's experience of the baptism of the Spirit (Acts 2) was interpreted as a continuation of Jesus' mission in the power of the Spirit. "Signs and wonders" attested their participation in the *now* but *not yet* of the inbreaking of the reign of God. Joel 2:28-29 was interpreted as the *end* time promise — "the beginning of the end." The early church saw itself as an eschatological community, the Spirit's outpouring gathered in a royal community, the community of the Spirit.[41] Roger Stronstad states that

> if we have interpreted Luke's Pentecostal narrative correctly, then the gift of the Spirit is not salvation, but it is for witness and service. In other words, with the transfer of the Spirit to the disciples on the day of Pentecost, they became a charismatic community, heirs to the earlier charismatic ministry of Jesus.[42]

While the church is not the reign of God, yet, as the community of the Spirit — where the Spirit manifests itself in a unique and particular way (Rom. 8:23; 1 Cor. 6:19; Eph. 2:14-18) — it has the purpose to both reflect and witness to the values of the reign, by the power of the Spirit to the world. Orlando Costas states it this way:

> Therefore, the church, which is *not* the Kingdom, is nevertheless its most *visible expression* and its most *faithful interpreter* in our age . . . as the community of believers from all times and places, the church both *embodies* the Kingdom in its life and *witnesses* to its presence and future in its mission.[43]

---

41. See James W. Jones, *The Spirit and the World* (New York: Hawthorn Books, 1975), pp. 51-76.

42. Stronstad, *Charismatic Theology,* p. 62. Stronstad defines the term *charismatic* in a functional and dynamic sense. "By 'charismatic' I mean God's gift of His Spirit to His servants, either individually or collectively, to anoint, empower, or inspire them for divine service" (p. 13). It is thus devoid of soteriological connotations, emphasizing the prophetic and vocational.

43. Orlando Costas, *The Integrity of Mission: The Inner Life and Outreach of the Church* (New York: Harper and Row, 1979), p. 8 (italics his).

The church as the community of the Spirit is engaged in "spiritual power encounters." It struggles with the forces of sin and death, with the demonic powers that be, whether individually or institutionally manifested and whether morally, physically, or spiritually expressed. The church can depend on the *Parakletos* to bring the charismatic renewal of the church *in* and *for* the world. "Signs and wonders" are thus legitimate expectations in the Spirit's total liberation. Orlando Costas eloquently states the significance of the cosmic and historic "power encounter" in the following:

> The Kingdom is an indication of God's transforming presence in history . . . a symbol of God's transforming power, of his determination to make "all things new" (Rev. 21:5). The Kingdom of God stands for a new order of life: the new humanity and the new creation which have become possible through the death and resurrection of Jesus. This new order includes reconciliation with God, neighbor and nature, and, therefore, participation in a new world. It involves freedom from the power of sin and death, and, consequently, the strength to live for God and humanity. It encompasses the hope of a more just and peaceful moral order, and thus it is a call to vital engagement in the historical struggles for justice and peace.[44]

THE CHALLENGE TO CONFRONT
STRUCTURAL SIN AND EVIL

The Spirit's power encounter defines the cosmic struggle being waged for God's creation. The tendency of many is to see this struggle too individualistically and not see that spiritual warfare must correspond with the geography of evil — the sinful and evil structures of society. The evangelical church must see itself not only as a *locus* for personal liberation but also as a *locus* for social liberation. We must see that the texture of social living makes no easy distinctions between the personal and the social. The church's mission includes engaging in power encounters with sinful and evil structures.

44. Ibid., p. 6.

Our confrontation responds to the nature of the structures themselves. On the one hand, we are aware of their creatureliness — they are institutions and structures *by* and *for* humans, although their reality is *sui generis*. On the other hand, we are aware of their possible demonic nature — the "powers." On one level of the struggle, it means that the church must bring to bear, through our witness and labors, the power of the Spirit to break the chains of hate, hostility, and injustice embedded in them by introducing the values of the reign (i.e., love, justice, fair play) and setting in place a "chain of change"[45] that immediately (thus, radical change — revolution) or gradually (thus, multiple and cumulative amelioration — reformation) humanizes these structures and institutions. On the other level of the struggle, the church must witness to the demonic powers that lie behind the scene, by reminding them of their defeat in Christ and the coming New Age. This witness must be in the power of the Spirit, armed with the "full armor of God" (Eph. 6:10-18). Jim Wallis states it well:

> The church demonstrates Christ's victory over the powers by reminding them of their created role as servants, rebuking them in their idolatrous role as rulers, and resisting them in their totalitarian claims and purposes. . . . We are not asked to defeat the powers. That is the work of Christ, which he has already done and will continue to do. Our task is to be witnesses and signs of Christ's victory by simply standing firmly in our faith and belief against the seduction and slavery of the powers.[46]

The proclamation of Christ until he comes and its impact on urban society will be predicated on evangelicals constructing a theology and ethics of the Spirit that are consistent with Scripture and social reality — a theology of the Spirit that leads to a social spirituality, the missing dimension of evangelical spirituality.

As an evangelical Pentecostal, I challenge the Pentecostal and charismatic churches to go beyond the given theology of the second

---

45. See Mel King, *Chain of Change: Struggles for Black Community Development* (Boston: South End, 1981).

46. Wallis, *Agenda*, pp. 48-49.

person of the Trinity to develop a full-blown *pneumatology*,[47] the basis for an authentic and biblical spirituality. Perhaps, this may be our greatest contribution to the church as it approaches the twenty-first century. Maranatha!

47. See Eldin Villafañe, *The Liberating Spirit: Toward an Hispanic American Pentecostal Social Ethic* (Grand Rapids: Eerdmans, 1993).

CHAPTER 3

The Power of the Powerless: A Paradigm of Partnership from the Underside

But we preach Christ crucified: a stumbling block to Jews and foolishness to Gentiles, but to those whom God has called, both Jews and Greeks, Christ the power of God and the wisdom of God. For the foolishness of God is wiser than man's wisdom, and the weakness of God is stronger than man's strength.

1 CORINTHIANS 1:23-25, NIV

But he said to me, "My grace is sufficient for you, for my power is made perfect in weakness." Therefore I will boast all the more gladly about my weaknesses, so that Christ's power may rest on me. That is why, for Christ's sake, I delight in weaknesses, in insults, in hardships, in persecutions, in difficulties. For when I am weak, then I am strong.

2 CORINTHIANS 12:9-10, NIV

Several years ago (October 1978) Václav Havel wrote a very influential essay entitled "The Power of the Powerless."[1] Recently Francis Fukuyama, in his book *The End of History and the Last Man,* devoted a full chapter to the theme of "The Power of the Powerless."[2] Both highlight the underlying theme of legitimate power and its source in those persons perceived to be powerless by the greater society.

These authors underline a truth witnessed to by Scripture from Genesis to Revelation. Gustavo Gutiérrez expounds this truth in his work *The Power of the Poor in History,*[3] namely, that the locus of real power for significant change in history often lies not in the center of "real politiks," but in the "periphery" — with the oppressed — with those from the underside of history.

I want to challenge you by presenting some lessons learned from the "other partner" — those from the underside. These are the "poor" and "powerless" churches in our *barrios* and inner cities. In the church from the underside there is a model for us, a "Koinonia (or partnership) in the Spirit"[4] that is critical for the life and mission of the dominant church. This "Koinonia in the Spirit" is a story worth telling — it is a gift, a paradigm for our instruction.

I will focus my remarks on reflection mostly based on the church I know best — the Hispanic church in the *barrio.* Yet, I am sufficiently confident that the old dictum is still true: "You get to the universal through the particular." My theme falls under two major headings: "Partnership and the Cross" and "Paradigms from the Underside."

1. Václav Havel, "The Power of the Powerless," in *Open Letters: Selected Writings, 1965–1990* (New York: Knopf, 1991), pp. 125-214.

2. Francis Fukuyama, "The Power of the Powerless," in *The End of History and the Last Man* (New York: Free Press, 1992), pp. 254-65.

3. Gustavo Gutiérrez, *The Power of the Poor in History* (Maryknoll, N.Y.: Orbis, 1983).

4. See esp. J. Paul Sampley, *Pauline Partnership in Christ: Christian Community and Commitment in Light of Roman Law* (Philadelphia: Fortress, 1980), p. 60.

Partnership and the Cross

The major theme of this Congress on Urban Ministry is partnership. Partnership has many definitions. It is a richly nuanced word. Yet it is my deep conviction that partnership cannot be understood or practiced if it is not defined and informed by the cross. For it is at the cross of Christ that our personal and congregational self-centeredness is dealt with — thus freeing us up to give ourselves to "the other," from whatever culture, class, or color that "other" may be. The cross frees us up to enter into legitimate and authentic mutuality — true "Koinonia"!

It is at the cross of Christ that paradoxically our poverty and powerlessness are transvaluated into the power of God for personal and social transformation. The cross of our Lord Jesus Christ is not only a historical reality that is crucial to our theological self-understanding and experience of redemption, but it is also a paradigm — a model — for our lives and for the life of the church — especially if it is to play a redemptive and revitalizing role in the urban world.

The cross was, and is, the height of disgrace, futility, and power-lessness. Yet, this foolishness of God is wiser than the wisdom of the world, this "weakness of God is stronger than man's strength" (1 Cor. 1:25). This is part of the mystery of redemption — that an instrument of powerlessness becomes the ultimate expression in Christ of "the power of God and the wisdom of God" (1 Cor. 1:24).

In the personal life of the apostle Paul there is an experience, the truth of which not only serves to console the believer, but serves by analogous theological extension as a vital paradigm for the church.

> But he said to me, "My grace is sufficient for you, *for my power is made perfect in weakness.*" Therefore, I will boast all the more gladly about my weakness, so that Christ's power may rest on me. That is why, for Christ's sake, I delight in weaknesses, in insults, in hardships, in persecutions, in difficulties. *For when I am weak, then I am strong.* (2 Cor. 12:9-10, NIV)

When I look for models of vital, growing, and faithful Christianity around the world, I find them not in those churches whose life and mission are defined by the powers of this world. Rather, I look to the many "poor" churches — the churches from the underside — who by intention (explicit conformity to the gospel) or by oppression (implicit conformity to the gospel) bear the marks of the cross.

The church from the underside is the church of the cross — the cross is both its present experiential reality and its redemptive *modus operandi*. It is in the church of the cross that God's power is manifested, yes, perfected in weakness!

A Paradigm from the Underside

My prayer is that we might be reminded or perhaps learn anew, but most of all be challenged, to reappropriate some of the simple but fundamental truths that make for a true "Koinonia (or partnership) of the Spirit."

As a Hispanic — more specifically, as a Puerto Rican — I have seen and lived the vitality of the Hispanic church in the *barrios*. It is a church of the cross! In many ways this story is similar to many African-American churches in the inner city — similar to the many "churches of the poor" across the urban landscape of America and the world.

The Hispanic Protestant church is a church of an oppressed ethnic minority, one that lives and works under a dominant church and society. Yet, it is a church that in its most active and socially significant expressions plays for Hispanics, and models for society at large, the following five significant roles:

- Salvation: "A Liberated and Liberating Community"
- Social Service and Social Justice Provider
- Survival: "A Place of Cultural Survival and Affirmation"
- Secrets of the Reign: "Hermeneutical Advantage of the Poor"
- Signpost: "A Signpost of Protest, Resistance, and Priestly Presence"

These five "S's" should give us a snapshot of a church from the underside and a paradigm for our instruction.

Salvation: "A Liberated and Liberating Community"

Literally dotting the many inner-city *barrios* of America are communities of hope and liberation. The Hispanic church can be found in a storefront or a converted synagogue, or perhaps a traditional church building "abandoned" by its "sister" Anglo church. There one finds a simple but powerful proclamation of the gospel of Jesus Christ and the gathering of God's church, providing a community of "freedom," "dignity," "self-worth," "comfort," "strength," "hope," "joy" — "abundant life."

Orlando Costas is right when he states:

> Indeed the prophetic genius of the minority church is that it has learned to "sing the Lord's song in a strange land" (Psalms 137:4). It has been able to give its respective communities a vision of a more fraternal, just, and peaceful world, enabling them to hope even when there seems to be no hope. Its ethic has been clearly one of liberation.[5]

As a liberated community, the Hispanic church lives out the gospel both in its life and in its liberating mission. Though poor by the standards of the world, it witnesses to a richness of faith, hope, and love (1 Cor. 13:13).

"For when I am weak, then I am strong"!

Social Service and Social Justice Provider

Without a doubt, in the *barrios* the Hispanic Protestant church plays a vital role in providing critically needed social services, and in many cases, social justice advocacy.

In a study on the Hispanic community, sociologists Melvin Delgado and Denise Humn-Delgado emphasize the significant role played by Hispanic religious institutions. Most noteworthy was their positive

---

5. Orlando Costas, "Social Justice in the Other Protestant Tradition: A Hispanic Perspective," in *Contemporary Ethical Issues in the Jewish and Christian Traditions,* ed. Frederick Greenspahn (Hoboken, N.J.: Ktau, 1986), p. 224.

description of Hispanic Pentecostalism in the *barrios*. The following
description from Vivian Garrison's "Sectarianism and Psychological Ad-
justment: A Controlled Comparison of Puerto Rican Pentecostals and
Catholics," cited by the Delgados, is both typical and cogent: .

> Each of these small churches has a missionary society that answers
> requests of members and nonmembers, visits homes, and cares for
> the ill and disturbed. In addition to pastoral counseling, the ministries
> and the missionary societies provide emergency financial aid, go to
> the airport to meet new arrivals and orient them to the city, and locate
> housing and employment for members through the Pentecostal
> grapevine. All of these churches support several Pentecostal programs
> to rehabilitate drug addicts, prostitutes, and other outcasts of society.
> Most Pentecostals go to their ministers or members of their church
> with any problem they might have. Services offered by the church are
> provided from the resources within the group and within the broader
> network of Pentecostal affiliations.[6]

In the *barrios* the Hispanic Protestant church provides a network
of informal social services that goes a long way in coping and overcoming in an otherwise hostile and oppressive context.

"For when I am weak, then I am strong"!

Survival: "A Place of Cultural Survival and Affirmation"

The Hispanic church in the *barrios* has been the locus of cultural validation. Family values, language, music, art, custom, and symbols of Hispanic and Latino *pueblo* have been sustained, nourished, and affirmed
in the Hispanic church. When the dominant culture pressed for a forced
assimilation, many found their Hispanic culture and values safeguarded
in the enclaves of our Hispanic churches.

No one can visit a Hispanic Protestant church (particularly in-

---

6. Melvin Delgado and Denise Humn-Delgado, "Natural Support Systems: Source
of Strength in Hispanic Communities," *Social Work* (January 1982): 85.

digenous Pentecostal congregations) today without being impressed by the "fiesta" (celebration) expressed in their native instruments — guitar, maracas, and even bongos — and thus savor the depth of the Hispanic soul! The role of the fiesta in Hispanic American culture is deeply meaningful. Religious and nonreligious events in the calendar year mark the occasions that are the basis of a marvelous sense of community that celebrates life through fiesta.

Ruben Armendariz in his article "Hispanic Heritage and Christian Education" quotes Octavio Paz, who says that the fiesta "marks a return to the beginning, to the primordial state in which each one is united with the great all. Every true fiesta is religious because every true festival is communion."[7]

Virgilio Elizondo, in his book *Galilean Journey: The Mexican-American Promise*, makes "Fiesta" a central theological category. Though he speaks about Mexican-Americans, what he says can be applied equally to all Hispanic Americans:

> The happiness and joy . . . is immediately obvious to outsiders. The tragedies of their history have not obliterated laughter and joy . . . fiesta is the mystical celebration of a complex identity, the mystical affirmation that life is a gift and is worth living. . . . In the fiesta the Mexican-American rises above the quest for the logical meaning of life and celebrates the very contradictions that are the essence of the mystery of human life.[8]

It is in the many Hispanic churches in our *barrios* that many find their culture — their lives — affirmed. Amid the experience of oppression, domination, and the struggle for mere survival, the fiesta — with games and rituals, music and dance, food and "familia" — speaks eloquently of joy, hope, and life.

"For when I am weak, then I am strong"!

7. Octavio Paz, "Reflections," *The New Yorker*, November 17, 1979, quoted by Ruben P. Armendariz, "Hispanic Heritage and Christian Education," *ALERT* (November 1981): 26.

8. Virgilio Elizondo, *Galilean Journey: The Mexican-American Promise* (Maryknoll, N.Y.: Orbis, 1983), p. 43.

Secrets of the Reign: "Hermeneutical Advantage of the Poor"

As a church from the underside, the Hispanic church in the U.S.A. is a "church of the poor." Scripture teaches us, as has been made quite clear by Third World theology, especially that from Latin America, that God has a "preferential option for the poor." In the Law, Prophets, and the Gospels God's justice is demonstrated in God's preference for those whom society has discarded. Paul says it in no uncertain terms:

> But God chose the foolish things of the world to shame the wise; God chose the weak things of the world to shame the strong. He chose the lowly things of this world and the despised things — and the things that are not — to nullify the things that are. (1 Cor. 1:27-28, NIV)

When taken seriously, this "good news to the poor" that Jesus preached places the "non-poor" at a decided disadvantage. The witness of Scripture is clear that while the gospel is for all, the rich and powerful (including the religious "powers-that-be"), because of their grasping or dependence ("idolatry") on their financial or religious advantage, hear it as "bad news." This is part and parcel of the meaning of the "hermeneutical advantage of the poor."

One's understanding of the Scripture and of the faith is decidedly influenced by one's position regarding the "poor." There is a sense in which wealth and power blind one to see and to participate in God's liberating action in history. In another sense, the "poor" church is at an advantageous position to hear the secrets of the reign. Their dependence, their trust, their power is on the mercies of a just, loving, and speaking God.

Justo L. González states:

> What all this means is that when we understand the significance of the poor for the proper understanding of Scripture and of the Christian faith, we must come to the conclusion that a church that does not have the poor in its midst, a church that does not identify with the poor, is at a decided disadvantage.[9]

"For when I am weak, then I am strong"!

9. Justo González, *The Hispanic Ministry of the Episcopal Church in the Metropolitan Area of New York and Environs* (New York: Grants Program of Trinity Parish, 1985), p. 7.

Signpost: "A Signpost of Protest, Resistance, and Priestly Presence"

To the dominant church the Hispanic congregation is often a "foreign enclave," a possible "threat to the unity of the universal church," or a "mission station." This is a paternalistic view at best, one that is shattered by the persistent presence of the Hispanic church, which does not go away, but stands, in the words of Orlando Costas, "as a disturbing sign on the fringes of an unjust society . . . a prophetic indictment against the racism, political oppression, economic exploitation and sociocultural marginalization which have been such a constituent part of the American way of life."[10]

Costas underlines the ambivalent nature of a dominant church's interpretation and practice of the gospel — one compromised in its legitimation of the vested interest and institution of the powers that be, but yet compelled to come to terms with the *conditio sine qua non* of gospel faithfulness, namely, commitment to the poor and the oppressed. Thus the prophetic witness of the Hispanic church serves as "a sign of protest not only against an unjust society, but also against the legitimizing role of the majority church and its theological and social betrayal of the gospel."[11]

Let me state it a different way: The mere *presence* of the Hispanic church in the *barrios* is:

(1) *a prophetic witness* — to the principalities and powers, interpreted as either institutions and/or people who dehumanize God's children;

(2) *a prophetic witness* — to the other churches and denominations who have left or refuse to enter our *barrios;*

(3) *a prophetic witness* — to the *barrios* members themselves, who are challenged to forgiveness, hope, and community; and

(4) *a prophetic witness* — to the Hispanic believers themselves, who are challenged and called not to accept their "status quo."

The Hispanic church's presence as a priestly community in a deep and mysterious way sacralizes the *barrios,* providing space or context for the gathering of God's people for intercession, prayer, and strength.

10. Costas, "Social Justice," p. 223.
11. Ibid.

The Puerto Rican author Piri Thomas, referring to his Tía's (aunt's) Pentecostal church, speaks to this reality:

> It was a miracle how they could shut out . . . the . . . horrors of decaying rotten tenement houses and garbage-littered streets, with drugs running through the veins of our ghetto kids. It was a miracle that they could endure the indignities poured upon our "Barrios." I knew that every one of them didn't get weaker. They got stronger. Their prayers didn't get shorter. They got longer.[12]

"For when I am weak, then I am strong"!

Conclusion

The Hispanic church, as a church from the underside, lives out in the *barrios* for its Hispanic *pueblo* a model of true "Koinonia (or partnership) of the Spirit." It is in partnership with the hurting, the needy, the poor, and the oppressed in its midst. It is in partnership with the crucified God!

My challenge, the challenge of the Hispanic paradigm, is simple, but profound: To what degree are our denominations, our churches, our local congregations, expressions of true partnership with the poor — a partnership with the church from the underside? Does our partnership (not solidarity, for partnership is deeper and costlier) represent the cross?

- Is our partnership *with* the poor expressed in terms of a true liberated and liberating community?
- Is our partnership *with* the poor expressed in terms of a social service and social justice provider?
- Is our partnership *with* the poor expressed in terms of a *place* for culture, for human survival and affirmation?
- Is our partnership *with* the poor expressed in terms of a bearer of the secret of the kingdom?

12. Piri Thomas, *Savior, Savior, Hold My Hand* (Garden City, N.Y.: Doubleday, 1972), pp. 19-20.

• Is our partnership *with* the poor expressed in terms of a true signpost of protest, resistance, and priestly presence?

There is a price to be paid for this kind of partnership. It is not cheap grace, it is costly discipleship! It is partnership in the cross — which is perhaps not too popular today. Yet, I am reminded that the other side of the cross is the resurrection — for a theology of the cross (the power of the cross) lies in Easter Sunday. Ultimately, the resurrection is the *Power of the Powerless!*

Listen to Paul: "I want to know Christ and the power of his resurrection and the *fellowship of sharing in his suffering*" (Phil. 3:10a). This is fellowship/partnership or Koinonia of sharing in his suffering. It is no accident that in this verse resurrection precedes suffering. Ultimately — for Paul as for ourselves — we cannot really enter into a true Koinonia/ fellowship (a partnership of sharing in his suffering with others) if we have not and if we do not experience his resurrection power. The *Power of the Powerless* in our *barrios,* our ghettos, of the church from the underside is the power of the cross and the resurrection!

The "Koinonia (or partnership) in the Spirit" that the Scriptures challenge us to live in, by, and with is modeled to us by many historical expressions of the Lord's one church. Scripture teaches us, history demonstrates, and, I pray, the five "S's" of the Hispanic church's paradigm challenge us to see modeled the truth of the "Power of the Powerless" — to see that God's power is manifested, yes, perfected in weakness! When we have captured such a vision we will have entered into the "Koinonia (or partnership) of the Spirit" with the church of the underside.

Therefore, I will boast all the more gladly about my weakness, so that Christ's power may rest on me. That is why, for Christ's sake, I delight in weaknesses, in insults, in hardships, in persecutions, in difficulties. *For when I am weak, then I am strong.* (2 Cor. 12:9-10)

PART TWO

URBAN MINISTRY

CHAPTER 4

Patience and the City

My brethren, count it all joy when ye fall into divers temptations; knowing this, that the trying of your faith worketh patience. But let patience have her perfect work, that ye may be perfect and entire, wanting nothing.

JAMES 1:2-4, KJV

"Al amanecer, armado de una *ardiente paciencia* entraremos a las espléndidas ciudades" (At dawn, armed with a *burning patience* we shall enter the splendid cities). These were the words of Chilean poet Pablo Neruda, spoken at his acceptance of the Nobel Prize for Literature in 1971. These words were part of a speech entitled "Towards the Splendid City," in which he shared his burden and vision for the poetic and literary task.

Neruda spoke of the pilgrimage to the splendid city as one that is entered into, is achieved, armed with a "burning patience." Though Neruda's vision of the splendid city differs, perhaps quite radically, from ours, his words underscore the common path, the common quality or virtue needed to enter the city.

I will posit here that "burning patience" is a critical and indispensable virtue for effective ministry in our *not* too splendid cities.

Burning Patience and the Splendid City

In a biblical and theological sense this "burning patience" is nothing else than the believers' patience *(hupomone)* that James speaks of so eloquently in his epistle. It is the fruit of the Spirit.

Patience in Scripture is not a passive quality or virtue, it is not hopeless resignation — a "Qué será será." Rather, it is an active quality, a "burning virtue," that, captivated by an eschatological vision of God's heavenly city, can, in hope against hope, see signs of the splendid city manifested concretely, if but for short and imperfect moments in history, in our earthly city.

In other words, "burning patience" is that quality of faith that in any city — be it Los Angeles, New York, Chicago, or Boston — notwithstanding its complexity and confusion, its chaos and crime, its heart cries and challenges, *can* and *must* believe that the gospel of our Lord and Savior Jesus Christ makes a difference. It believes that in the "now and not yet" of the kingdom of God, one can believe in a city where there is comprehension and clarity, care and concern, consolation, justice, and love. In other words, there can be shalom — peace, harmony, and wholeness with justice.

This city — Boston — is our city. Armed with a "burning patience" we can bring to it a "measure of grace" from that splendid city for which our hearts yearn. The pattern, the model, the paradigm of the heavenly splendid city can begin to be drawn and applied to the diverse communities of our city.

We know, we do not have to be reminded by Augustine, that the heavenly city cannot be established by human hands — yet we know that on this side of the cross and empty tomb, the powers of the heavenly splendid city are ours! We know that we can by faith appropriate and implement what I have called "measures of grace" in our present evil world.

The gospel witness is clear and compelling: "the kingdom of heaven has been forcefully advancing, and forceful men lay hold of it" (Matt. 11:12, NIV; "los valientes lo arrebatan . . . el reino de los cielos está en tensión, y los esforzados lo arrebatan" — Nocar/Colunga).

The mystery and the glory of the gospel is not only that it offers hope for eternal life in the splendid city, but that it offers hope and grace in the present life, in our earthly city. Ours is not a "sinking boat" theology of the city, an escapist view favored by some of our fundamentalist friends. Neither is it a "love boat" theology of the city, one favored by our liberal friends. I would like to think that ours is a "transport boat" theology of the city. We neither despair of our city, nor dare we romanticize its possibilities. We nevertheless move on, amid storms and trials, carrying and seeking the shalom of the city. "And seek the shalom (peace) of the city whither I have caused you to be carried away captives, and pray unto the Lord for it: for in the shalom (peace) thereof shall ye have shalom (peace)" (Jer. 29:7, KJV).

Armed with a "burning patience," informed by the reality of sin and grace, and empowered by the Holy Spirit, we can indeed be a witness to and a reality of the splendid city.

BURNING PATIENCE AND HOPE IN THE CITY

It is my strong conviction that if we are to succeed in urban ministry, we must understand, we must appropriate, we must permit the Holy Spirit to work in us this virtue of "burning patience." "Burning patience" is that quality of faith which permits one to live in the "now and not yet," to live in the tension of the age to come and the present age. It is the quality of faith that gives meaning and strength to our present endeavors — to our present ministry. Trials and tribulations will come. Failures will be real. Yet, we have a vision of the splendid city. We know — we have a foretaste of heaven, the Spirit of God burns within us — we have hope, we can be patient. We have a "burning patience"!

There is a world out there, there is a community out there, there are people out there, there are individuals out there — destroyed, despondent, defeated by hopelessness. The dark side of the city, of any city, is hopelessness. We are challenged to share the gospel of our Lord Jesus Christ. By his Spirit, we are "to preach the gospel to the poor . . . to heal the brokenhearted, to preach deliverance to the captives, and recovering of sight to the blind, to set at liberty them that are bruised, to preach the acceptable year of the Lord" (Luke 4:18-19, KJV). To preach the whole gospel to the whole person! To bring hope where there is hopelessness!

On a more personal note, "burning patience" will be the virtue that will keep us from "running," from "giving up," when things do not go our way — when the church does not seem to grow, when the elders or church officials say no to our "beautiful" plans, when the church burns down suspiciously in a targeted development area, when the rent is due and we don't have the money, when the refrigerator is empty, when they discriminate against us, when they (or he or she) reject us.

"Burning patience" speaks to me and informs me that urban ministry requires time, commitment, fervor — in the biblical idiom, to be "filled with the Spirit" — for it is a long haul! We cannot enter the splendid city in *a* day. The Spirit of God does not produce his "measures of grace" in our earthly city in *a* day. We must be patient. We must work patiently — but not passively! The biblical concept of patience, "burning patience," is an apparent paradox. Our attitude and disposition, thus, must be like the one expressed by Napoleon to his valet: "¡Vísteme despacio que estoy de prisa!" ("Dress me slowly for I am in a hurry!")

We must have a "burning patience" — for "at dawn, armed with a burning patience we shall enter the splendid city."

▼ CHAPTER 5 ▼

An Approach to Winning
Ethnic Minorities in the City

THE ETHNIC REALITY

Invited and uninvited, rich and poor — but mostly poor — foreigners are pouring into the U.S. in greater numbers than at any time
since the last great surge of European immigrants in the early 1900's.
Indeed, the U.S. today accepts twice as many foreigners as the rest of
the world's nations combined. . . . Although their turn-of-the-centu-
ry predecessors were mainly Europeans, today's new arrivals are
mostly from Latin America and, to a lesser extent, Asia and the Caribbean. They are transforming the U.S. urban landscape into something
that it has not been for decades: a mosaic of exotic languages, faces,
customs, restaurants and religions. (*TIME*, May 18, 1981)

This mosaic of ethnicity is further enlarged when we consider the other
ethnic minorities in our midst. These represent, in the words of Thom
Hopler, "the nonvolunteer Immigrants,"[1] namely, the Indians (Native
Americans), Puerto Ricans, and the American Blacks.

The "mission field has come to us" is the statement we now hear.
I would add, "It has always been among us!"

---

1. Thom Hopler, *A World of Difference: Following Christ Beyond Your Cultural
Walls* (Downers Grove, Ill.: InterVarsity Press, 1981), p. 167.

Although ethnic minorities have been with us from our earliest history, and indeed the U.S.A. is a nation of immigrants, it has been only recently that we have looked to and affirmed the "cultural pluralism" of our nation.

The pressure for Americanization into the so-called melting pot has been graphically depicted by Robert Bellah in his essay, "Evil and the American Ethos." He says:

> For a festival sponsored by Henry Ford during the early 1920's a giant pot was built outside the gates of his factory. Into this pot danced groups of gaily dressed immigrants dancing and singing their native songs. From the other side of the pot emerged a single stream of Americans dressed alike in the contemporary standard dress and singing the national anthem. As the tarantellas and the polkas at last faded away only the rising strains of the national anthem could be heard as all the immigrants finally emerged. The enormous pressures which created this vast transformation amounted to a forced conversion.[2]

It has been made abundantly clear to anthropologists, historians, educators, and social scientists alike that the idea of Americanization or assimilation through the melting pot is a myth or at best for some a culture domination by white Anglo-Saxon Protestants.[3]

It has also been made abundantly clear that the obliteration of all ethnic distinctions is not a desirable or achievable reality for assimilation into the American way of life.

The contribution of the many ethnic groups in the U.S.A. has been the factor that has produced the American way of life. The ethnic groups and values have been and are a permanent asset in American life. In pluralistic America there has been and can continue to be a creative dynamic of ethnic diversity within national unity.

2. Robert Bellah, "Evil and the American Ethos," *Sanctions for Evil*, ed. Nevitt Sandord and Craig Comstock (San Francisco: Jossey-Bass, 1971), p. 181.

3. Nathan Glazer and Patrick Moynihan, *Beyond the Melting Pot* (Cambridge, Mass.: MIT Press, 1963); Milton M. Gordon, *Assimilation in American Life: The Role of Race, Religion and National Origins* (New York: Oxford Univ. Press, 1964); Michael Novak, *The Rise of the Unmeltable Ethnics: Politics and Culture in the Seventies* (New York: Macmillan, 1971).

The importance and validity of cultural pluralism, notwithstanding recent reservations raised by some about our latest immigrants, must be affirmed if we are to overcome the *curse of ethnocentrism*, and if we are to effectively witness to the transforming power of our Lord Jesus Christ among them and with the ethnic minorities in our midst.

Religious Experience and Cultural Reality

One's religious experience is mediated through one's cultural reality. The revelation of God in the Scriptures is identified and given in written, historical, and cultural realities. Without the particular ethnic background, the universal principles applicable to our time would be meaningless. The biblical witness respects and legitimizes the particular culture of the people in their religious quest.

When Christ comes to our lives, he does not come to destroy our ethnic or cultural identity. However, he will place a "leavening" in us to forge a new identity. For this reason, Paul concludes in Galatians 6:15, "For in Christ Jesus neither circumcision availeth anything, nor uncircumcision, but a new creature." In the same manner, before the reality of the new man all are relativized in Christ: "And have put on the new man . . . where there is neither Greek nor Jew, circumcision nor uncircumcision, Barbarian, Scythian, bond nor free: but Christ is all, and in all" (Col. 3:10-11, KJV).

But this relativizing of our different identities does not mean that they are not important, rather that they are submitted to Christ. What is indeed eliminated is the superiority of one over another and the possibility of imposing one identity on another. This was in part the struggle waged by Paul with the Judaizers who demanded circumcision, that is to say, a Jewish identity, in order for the Gentiles to become Christians.[4]

In the words of Bishop Mortimer Arias, "the Lord accepts the culture which gives shape to the human voice which responds to the voice of Christ."[5] One's religious experience is indeed mediated through one's cultural reality.

4. See Acts, chaps. 11 and 15, and Galatians.
5. Mortimer Arias, *Salvación es Liberación* (Buenos Aires: La Aurora, 1973), p. 77.

If we are to win ethnic minorities for Christ, we must uphold and affirm their ethnic and cultural identity. Our evangelistic outlook must be permeated by these basic cultural presuppositions. We can summarize them as follows: (1) the "worthiness" of each ethnic group; (2) the validity of cultural pluralism; and (3) the mediation of one's religious experience through one's cultural reality.

FOUR "E's" FOR WINNING ETHNIC MINORITIES FOR CHRIST

Moving from the considerations of some of the basic presuppositions needed to reach ethnic minorities for Christ and building upon them, let me suggest four "E's" for winning ethnic minorities for Christ. They are the following: (1) empowering of ethnic leadership; (2) evangelism that is wholistic; (3) education that is contextual; and (4) ecclesiastical structures that liberate.

Empowering of Ethnic Leadership

We must identify and empower the existing ethnic gospel witness or ministries. It is the height of "imperialistic evangelism" to *assume* automatically that there is no gospel witness among a particular ethnic group and that we are the ones to do it.

First and foremost, *identify* means prayer and reflection. It means seeking the Holy Spirit's guidance for *me* or *my* church to get involved in ethnic ministry. Is my community undergoing ethnic transition? When is the appropriate time to get involved with ethnic groups? Should only a member or a small group from our church be involved? Should we as a whole church be involved? Are we willing to sacrificially commit our resources and most of all ourselves to this outreach?

Second, *identify* means research and dialogue. Who is reaching out to this particular ethnic group in my community? Is there a Christian witness present? A church? A store front? A parachurch ministry? A radio or television outreach into this particular ethnic group? Maybe there is but a lone Christian family among them? Or perhaps a lone Christian worker among them?

Research and dialogue means learning as much as one can about this particular ethnic group. Much information can be gathered from community, civic, and religious agencies and institutions — be they social agencies, welfare and immigration offices, schools, police departments, libraries, or city halls. You should also try your local YMCA/YWCA and Salvation Army. Whether one's church gets involved directly or indirectly in ministry to an ethnic group, one should learn as much as possible about their history, culture, language, and religion. One should know and understand as much as possible about the "immigrant experience" — the uprootedness, the anomie and socioeconomic conditions impinging on the ethnic group. One should establish dialogue with individuals representing a particular ethnic group. Dialogue can lead to fruitful contact with existing community and/or Christian leaders.

It is my belief that one should venture out into direct ethnic ministry only after one (1) has gotten clearance from the Lord; (2) has found no gospel witness in that particular ethnic group; and (3) cannot associate with existing indigenous ethnic ministry — for reasons of doctrine and/or moral testimony.

If there is a gospel witness present in the community — be they Black Americans, Native Americans, Hispanics, Asians, etc. — we should do all we can to empower that ethnic leadership.

Empowering ethnic leadership means providing economic, political, material, educational, and human resources to the existing ethnic church. It is placing in their hands these resources with "no strings attached." It is giving and relating nonpaternalistically. It is sharing and opening to them the structures of power in our communities, and the nation as a whole, be they the political and governing agencies, the educational systems (secular or Christian), the denominational or religious institutions, committees, boards, or other decision-making bodies.

There is something to be said about the missiological concept of the "homogeneous unit principle." While I have certain reservations relative to this principle, let me make the following observations pertinent to it.

All things being equal, and sometimes even when they may not be, an indigenous ethnic leader has greater and far more lasting impact than an outsider, whether it be an Asian ministering in Chinatown, a Black in an inner-city Black or transitional community, or a Hispanic in "El Barrio."

I believe in cross-cultural missions, which is biblical and relevant. But I also believe that cross-cultural missionaries, whether in Africa or New York City, should work "with" and "under" existing indigenous gospel witness if present.

If we really want to win ethnic minorities for Christ, let us ask the Holy Spirit to guide us to where and with whom the Spirit is working so as to be truly co-laborers with God's Spirit.

Evangelism that Is Wholistic

In launching out to win and minister to ethnic minorities it is important to keep in mind the classical missiological categories of the church's mission, namely, (1) *Kerygma,* proclamation of the gospel, (2) *Koinonia,* the community or fellowship of the gospel believers, and (3) *Diaconia,* the service of the gospel.

We have placed in evangelical quarters the greatest emphasis on the Kerygma, especially in a verbal and individualistic mode. Today's inner-city and ethnic ministry often requires the manifestation of Diaconia and/or Koinonia as effective means and expressions of evangelization.

The majority of our ethnic minorities are found in our great cities. As our cities go, so go our ethnic minorities. By virtue of their poverty and disenfranchisement, our ethnic families are found in the inner cities of our metropolitan centers. The health and welfare of ethnic minorities is tied to the health and welfare of our cities.

The "rediscovery" and interest in urban ministry in the past few years by the evangelical establishment promises to be an excellent opportunity for winning ethnic minorities. We must realize, though, that ministering in the inner city requires a "wholistic gospel." This is best expressed to me by the word *peace.* We are reminded in Scripture to "seek the peace of the city" (Jer. 29:7). That captive and pilgrim community in Jeremiah was challenged to seek the peace (welfare) of the city. We can do no less if we also are to experience the promise, "for in the peace thereof shall ye have peace."

Peace (shalom) is a rich word. The word and its derivatives are found (not counting proper names) more than 350 times in the Old Testament. In the New Testament usage its total meaning is not exhausted by the Greek *(eirene)* or for that matter by our English *peace.* It is in the Old Testament root meaning of shalom that we find its richness and the significant meaning of "completeness," "wholeness," "soundness," and "welfare." It speaks of harmony and concord — it is a wholistic term — responding to needs of the whole person.

The essence of the gospel is shalom. In Christ peace has come (Luke 1:79; 2:14, 29f.), by him it is bestowed (Mark 5:34; Luke 7:50; John 20:19, 21, 26), and his disciples are its messengers (Luke 24:45ff.). We are exhorted by Paul in Ephesians 6:15 to "have your feet shod with the equipment of the gospel of peace." In the book of Acts in the encounter of Peter with Cornelius we are told of "preaching good news of peace by Jesus Christ, He is Lord of all" (Acts 10:36). Peace between humans is part of the purpose for which Christ died (Ephesians 2) and of the Spirit's work (Gal. 5:22), and humans must also be active to promote it (Eph. 4:3; Heb. 12:14f.).

Shalom speaks of the mission of "today's Church — a community of exiles and pilgrims." Seeking the peace of the city means to seek (1) peace in the community (it is Koinonia), (2) peace (welfare) of others — compassion/concern for all people, but above all for the poor and the needy (it is Diaconia), and (3) peace (wholeness and harmony) — it speaks about reconciliation among races and ethnic groups and above all reconciliation with God (it is Kerygma). It is preaching, "be ye reconciled to God."

Education that Is Contextual

If we are to win ethnic minorities for Christ, we must provide an ethnic approach to Christian education and Christian literature. This involves a conscious concern to accent the characteristics of a given ethnic group by making prominent its history, culture, values, and beliefs. It means our curriculum should be consistent with the goals of a multiethnic and multicultural society. Teachers and curriculum within church schools serve as primary instruments for responding to the diverse needs of learners in a pluralistic society.

In the words of the Reverend Joe Nash of the Black Christian Educational Resource Center, "If you affirm the value of an ethnic approach, it is clear that a distinction should be made between educational models that function to emancipate (education for liberation) or enslave (education for conformity)."[6]

If we are to win ethnic minorities for Christ, we must also provide for contextual theological education for ethnic leaders and for those who would minister among them. I am thinking here of a theological education consistent with the philosophical approach of TEE (Theological Education by Extension). All TEE programs need not be the same. Its central philosophy can be applied in the U.S.A. among ethnic minorities.

There must be a commitment by our churches, denominations, Bible institutes, colleges, and seminaries to consider seriously reaching out and establishing theological centers in ethnic communities for the training of ethnic minority leadership.

There are a number of seminaries responding to this challenge. Among them is Gordon-Conwell Theological Seminary's Center for Urban Ministerial Education located in Boston, Massachusetts.[7] The curriculum projections for the next academic year will feature courses in English (for Black Americans and Anglos), Spanish (for Hispanics), French (for Haitians), and Portuguese (for Cape Verdians and Brazilians). It thus seeks to respond to the multiethnic leadership of the greater Boston area.

Many of our ethnic communities have produced outstanding natural leadership. These leaders are quite capable of serious theological study within the context of their family, work, community, and church responsibilities.

Ecclesiastical Structures that Liberate

If we are to win ethnic minorities for Christ, we must provide the proper church structures to "house" ethnic minorities. I refer here to the ap-

6. Joe Nash, "Multiethnic Ministries," *Black Guard* no. 2 (Black Christian Education Resources Center; Winter 1978): 1.

7. Rudy Mitchell and Eldin Villafañe, "The Center for Urban Ministerial Education: A Case Study in Theological Education by Extension," *New England Journal of Ministry* 1, no. 2 (March 1981).

propriate models for churches ministering or desiring to minister to ethnic groups in a community undergoing ethnic transitions.

David Sanchez's paper, "Viable Models for Churches in Communities Experiencing Ethnic Transition,"[8] provides us a four-point model worth considering.

The first model is the "multi-congregational model." According to Sanchez this pattern is "as a corporation composed of several congregations (Anglo and ethnic) in which the autonomy of each congregation is preserved and the resources of the congregations are combined to present a strong evangelistic witness in the community."[9]

The second model is the "temporary sponsorship model." This model pictures an Anglo congregation using its resources to minister to the ethnic groups in the neighborhood by aiding them to establish their own ethnic congregation. It is the appropriate model for a dwindling Anglo congregation when there is little or no chance of it surviving in the long run.

The third model is the "bi-lingual, bi-cultural model." This is an "integrated church" model, where members of more than one homogeneous unit hold membership and participate in the activities of a single local congregation.

The fourth model is the "total transition model." This pattern involves the planned phasing out of the original congregation and the phasing in of a new ethnic neighborhood congregation. Sanchez states that this works best when "there is a strong conviction that this will continue to be the Lord's church in that community — even though it has taken on a different cultural clothing."[10]

The above models and others that can be added represent structural adaptations that try to respond to communities undergoing ethnic transitions. While the "multi-congregational model" may be the ideal for urban ministries in transitional communities, the other models are viable options. The particular *context of ministry,* with its distinct demo-

8. David Sanchez, "Viable Models for Churches in Communities Experiencing Ethnic Transition" (paper, Fuller Theological Seminary, 1976), in C. Peter Wagner, *Our Kind of People: The Ethical Dimensions of Church Growth in America* (Atlanta: John Knox, 1979), pp. 159-63.

9. Ibid., p. 159.

10. Ibid., p. 163.

graphic trends, cultural/ethnic diversity, and socioeconomic reality, coupled with the "health" of the receiving and the original church, are the most determinative factors in the Spirit-led selection of the appropriate model.

We need to reflect seriously and pray so that the ecclesiastical structures that would "house" ethnic minorities be ones that provide for their full affirmation, growth, and freedom — structures that liberate!

Conclusions

Winning ethnic minorities for Christ demands a contextual and cross-cultural sensitivity (1) for the empowering of ethnic leadership; (2) for an evangelism that is wholistic; (3) for an education that is contextual; and (4) for ecclesiastical structures that liberate.

If the churches of our Lord Jesus Christ are to play a significant role in our great cities among their ethnic minorities, they must be ready, in the words of C. Peter Wagner, "to include on their agendas some kind of program or activity that brings them into regular contact with Christian brothers and sisters of other homogeneous units. Only by taking steps to institutionalize this cross-cultural experience can the full implications of Christian love in a pluralistic society be made manifest to the world."[11]

11. Ibid.

CHAPTER 6

Hispanic and African-American Racial Reconciliation: A "Latin Jazz" Note

Tito Puentes, the legendary Latino musician, was performing with his band in Cambridge, near Boston. My wife Margie, my son Eldin, his fiancée Marlena, and I were right there — a front row table, no less! It was fascinating: the beat, the rhythm — the fusion of Afro-Cuban, jazz, blues, and other music influences that is now called "Latin Jazz." Not only Hispanics listen to Latin Jazz — it's now a crossover, as African Americans and Anglos enjoy it, too. As Cornel West notes, speaking about popular music, yet so apropos here, "the result is often a shared cultural space where some humane interaction takes place."[1]

The more I listened, the more it dawned on me that here we truly have an expression, a metaphor, for unity within diversity — for Shalom (peace) in race relations in the city. I could not get away from the realization that this musical expression — "Latin Jazz" — was not only celebrating a true harmony of the contributions of people of all colors, but was also being used by the Spirit! As a prophetic witness, albeit a "secular" one, it seems to me to challenge the church to a biblical posture of "racial Shalom" (peace — with its rich biblical meanings of healing, harmony, reconciliation, welfare, wholeness, and justice). It is a prophetic challenge to the church to be the "space" where the presence and contribution of believers of all colors could be seen as "light" and could

1. Cornel West, *Race Matters* (Boston, Mass.: Beacon, 1993), p. 84.

be savored as "salt" in a broken world. It is a prophetic challenge to the church to be a sign of the kingdom of God — a place where transformed relations and the presence of justice could be modeled.

Before this "Latin Jazz" occurs in our church and in our cities we need to understand a little of the informing sources of its rhythms. African Americans need to know more about Hispanics. Hispanics need to know more about African Americans. Anglos and others need to know more of both! Understanding our commonalities and differences is prerequisite to reconciliation and celebration.

CULTURAL HYBRIDITY — COMMONALITY AND DIFFERENCE

There is a culturally hybrid character to Hispanics' and African Americans' lives. Speaking of the hybrid character of black life, Cornel West reminds us that "the complex mixture of African, European, and Amerindian elements are constitutive of something that is new and black in the modern world."[2] For Hispanics the hybridity is also one of European (Spaniards), Amerindian, and African.

These three root streams or three distinct strands converge to provide the cultural heritage of Hispanics — they are clues to Hispanic identity. Hispanic cultural traits and value orientations thus emerge from this historical and biological convergence. While in some the Amerindian strand is more noticeable (Mexican and Central Americans), and in others the African (Dominican, Puerto Rican — i.e., the Caribbean), all have been deeply impacted by the Spaniard. The Spanish language and Christian religion (mostly Catholic, though increasingly Protestant) and its subsequent cultural development define all Hispanics.

To many Hispanics the pride of this "mestizaje" (mixed, hybrid) is eloquently noted by Don Pedro Albizu Campos:

> That there is African blood, I too carry it in my veins and I carry it with the supreme pride of human dignity. We have here Indian blood. . . . I too have Indian blood and because of that I feel perfectly

2. Ibid., p. 101.

American, indigenous American. . . . That there is white blood in us? I too carry it in my veins. . . . We are an historically predestined people, because Puerto Rico is the first nation in the world where the unity of the spirit with the biological unity of the body takes form.[3]

Yet, given this rich "mestizaje," many Hispanics find it difficult to adjust to North American culture's sharp racial distinctions. Clara Rodríguez, although speaking specifically of Puerto Ricans, underlines the predicament of all "mixed races" — while at the same time implicitly affirming the "mestizo's" unique culture:

> There are only two options open in biracial New York — to be white or black. These options negate the cultural existence of Puerto Ricans and ignore their insistence on being treated, irrespective of race, as a culturally intact group. Thus, U.S. racial attitudes necessarily make Puerto Ricans either white or black, attitudes and culture make them neither white nor black, and our own resistance and struggle for survival places us between whites and blacks. . . .
>
> Historically, Puerto Ricans arriving in New York have found themselves in a situation of perpetual incongruence — that is, they saw themselves differently than they were seen. . . . Puerto Ricans, a culturally-homogeneous, racially integrated group, find themselves opposed to the demand that they become racially divided and culturally "cleansed" of being Puerto Rican.[4]

Rodríguez's words are important for understanding Hispanics — not just Puerto Ricans. While it must be said that "racism" does exist among Hispanics themselves, it is not to be compared to the morally and spiritually reprehensible racism experienced by Hispanics at the hand of the dominant culture. Hispanics, like African Americans, have experienced at the hand of the white dominant culture "psychic scars and personal wounds now inscribed in the souls of black folk."[5] A subtle,

3. Pedro Albizu Campos, *La Conciencia Nacional Puertorriqueña* (Mexico, D.F.: Siglo Veintiuno, 1974), pp. 195-96.

4. Clara Rodríguez, "Puerto Rican: Between Black and White," in *The Puerto Rican Struggle*, ed. Clara Rodríguez et al. (New York: Puerto Rican Migration Research Consortium, 1980), pp. 25, 28.

5. West, *Race Matters*, p. 85.

but equally destructive, form of racism that many Hispanics experience can be illustrated by a parent in the Boston school busing crisis of recent history. She did not want to support busing, but she did not want to oppose it either. For you see, one of her children was "white," while the other was "black." She just wanted to be treated as a Puerto Rican — a culturally intact group, a racially integrated group.

CONTEXT AND CONFLICT

It is important to note that Hispanics were here before the Mayflower landed. Much of the Southwest and West was speaking Spanish and eating "tacos" before the English language became our patrimony. It is equally important to acknowledge the distinct waves of immigrants coming from Mexico, Puerto Rico, Cuba, the Caribbean, and Central and South America, mostly in the second half of this century.

According to the Census Bureau there are officially 22.4 million U.S. Hispanics. The 1980 figures noted 14.6 million Hispanics. But the 22.4 million (1990 figures) omitted approximately 3.5 million (the population of Puerto Rico, whose citizens have been U.S. citizens since 1917), plus the 2 to 4 million undocumented, plus undercount for improperly identified non-Hispanics, which would result in an estimate ranging from 25 million to 30 million Hispanics. By all conservative estimates, Hispanics will outnumber African Americans early in the next century.

Demographics only tell part of the story. Significant socioeconomic changes have occurred in the 1980s and 1990s in the U.S.A. In the words of Alex Prud'Homme, "Once solidly united in the drive for equality, blacks and Hispanics are now often at odds over such issues as jobs, immigration and politics."[6] Relations between Hispanics and African Americans are not good. In a society in which, since the past decade, the rich have been getting richer and the poor have been getting poorer in greater numbers, African Americans and Hispanics, given their socioeconomic status, have been left at the bottom to fight for survival.

The perception that Hispanics, particularly new immigrants, have taken away jobs from African Americans has been challenged. According

6. Alex Prud'Homme, "Race Relations: Brown vs. Black," *TIME*, July 29, 1993.

to a report by *TIME* magazine, "In Los Angeles County, for example, blacks, who make up 10% of the population, hold 30% of the county jobs. Hispanics, who constitute 33% of the population, hold only 18% of the jobs."[7] Of course statistics only tell part of the story, too. The real story is the plight of both African Americans and Hispanics in this society.

The Los Angeles riot — "rebellion" — must be seen in a context of fractured dreams of equal justice and frustrated hope of prosperity. It must also be seen as a struggle for power within a system dominated by white/Anglo Americans. The American dream is not working as it should, and that is putting it lightly. Sixty percent of the L.A. looters arrested were Hispanics, mostly all Central Americans (and a good number of them were deported), and 10 percent of those arrested were white! By some estimates, up to 40 percent of the businesses destroyed were owned by Hispanics. The Korean community in South Central L.A. was shaken by the riot — their financial loss was great. Lost also by all was the sense of civility, a fragile one that existed nevertheless. The picture is ugly. Were the L.A. riots foreshadowing a crisis that William Parnell calls "The Coming Race Wars"?

My son Dwight, who has taken four years of Chinese in high school and college, reminds me that the word *crisis* in Chinese, in their ideographic language, is composed of two words, one meaning "danger" and the other "opportunity." I cannot help but think that such is the situation that we face in America. No action or token action by the church will spell "danger." Yet a "hope-full" response by the church in our cities, across this land, will be an "opportunity" to witness to the Shalom of the kingdom. It will reveal the gospel of Jesus Christ as relevant to the affairs of this world. It will reveal a church that is faithful to biblical reconciliation and justice.

The Hope — Reconciliation and Celebration in a "Latin Jazz" Beat

What are the "rhythms" needed that can highlight the interplay of individuality and unity of African Americans and Hispanics? Let me make several suggestions.

7. Ibid.

First, we must establish lines of *racial discourse*. We must sit together and be truth-tellers even if it hurts. We must, in Christlike fashion, speak the truth in love. We need to be self-critical and nondogmatic. We must share our journey — our struggles and our victories. We must tell each other, and others who would listen, race-transcending narratives.

There are precedents for such dialogues. A noteworthy one was the April 1993 gathering of Black Pentecostal and Hispanic American Pentecostal Scholars Dialogue, sponsored by the Graymoor Ecumenical & Interreligious Institute, at Douglaston, New York. This dialogue was convened by Dr. David Daniels and myself. In an open and candid spirit we, the nine persons present, shared our "journeys" and emphasized the urgency of addressing the crying needs of African Americans and Hispanics in the city by means of our scholarship.

In Boston I have spoken with Dr. Michael Haynes, pastor of the historic 12th Baptist Church, about convening African-American and Hispanic pastors and leaders to the table. Our prayer is that through honest, frank discussion and joint works, projects of racial healings will emerge, impacting the greater community as well. Perhaps it is time for meetings such as these to take place in all of our major cities.

Second, we must identify and develop a *"new cadre" of leaders* in our community. The either/or battle of evangelism vs. social action is passé — it was never really ours. The new leadership, pastors and laypersons, must embrace a wholistic understanding of the gospel — a gospel that in the words of Martin Luther King, Jr., "at its best deals with the whole man, not only his soul but also his body, not only his spiritual well-being but also his material well-being."[8] We have excellent models, for example, in the work done by the John M. Perkins Foundation for Reconciliation & Development, the Christian Community Development Association (CCDA), and the Emmanuel Gospel Center in Boston.

In the Boston area we also have a vibrant model in the Center for Urban Ministerial Education (CUME) of Gordon-Conwell Theological Seminary. For eighteen years it has been providing urban leadership training. Every year over 300 students — pastors and church leaders —

8. Martin Luther King, Jr., *Strength to Love* (London: Collins and Sons, 1963), p. 150.

are taught in five languages: English, Spanish, French (for Haitians), Portuguese (for Brazilians), and American Sign Language for the deaf. Over 150 distinct churches from over 20 nationalities are represented at the center. By studying together and by meeting at their respective churches and communities, they demonstrate the Shalom of the kingdom of God. By applying a wholistic understanding of the gospel in the city, they demonstrate the relevancy and power of the gospel of Jesus Christ.

Finally, we must *confess* and *celebrate*. Confession is a prerequisite to celebration. It is a soft yet vital note in the rhythmic swing of our urban spirituality. We must transcend the bitter animosity of past wrongs. We must forgive and realize that our fight is not against "white" or "brown" or "black" — "but against principalities, against powers, against the rulers of the darkness of this world, against spiritual wickedness in high places" (Eph. 6:12).

Celebration is the high key. Celebration — our Hispanic "fiesta" — is part and parcel of who we are! Let us celebrate by building coalitions of evangelistic and social outreach in our cities that will reflect that multicultural group around the throne of the Lamb in the book of Revelation. Let us celebrate through pulpit exchange, through visiting one another's churches, and by coming together in church or at other civic functions to be inspired and challenged by the "heroes" of our faith and history.

"Latin Jazz" is quite a beat — a challenging metaphor for all of us to reflect the unity among the diversity of the body of Christ.

CHAPTER 7

The Sociocultural Matrix of Intergenerational Dynamics: An Agenda for the 1990s

MATRIX OF INTERGENERATIONAL DYNAMICS: SETTING OUR PARAMETERS

What do we mean by the word *matrix?* There are various understandings or definitions of this word. Etymologically we can understand it well in Spanish by one word, *Matriz* or *womb*. Biologically, then, the matrix or *matriz* is where the "fetus" or "baby" is formed. It is the "womb" that in those early stages of life provides a context of integrated neural, chemical, and other biological networks that informs and forms that baby to be.

In an analogous fashion we can best understand intergenerational issues if we are informed by the sociocultural matrix that gives it birth, develops it, and nurtures it. So when I speak about the sociocultural matrix of intergenerational dynamics, I am interested in placing and defining that context which forms and informs intergenerational reality.

THREE "C's" OR THREE BASIC
CATEGORIES/ELEMENTS IN MATRIX

There are three basic categories ("C's") that are elements of this matrix: (1) Cultural/social reality; (2) communication/language; and (3) the church.

Cultural/Social Reality

There are three "root streams" or distinct strands that converge to provide the cultural heritage of Hispanics: the Spanish (European), the Amerindian, and the African. The cultural traits and value orientations that emerge from this historical and biological convergence provide what I have noted in my writings as the ideal type or profile·of "Homo Hispanicus" (passion, personalism, sense of community, fiesta, particular sense of family, and other values and traits).

The scope of this essay does not permit me to elaborate, but suffice it to say in passing that this first *mestizaje* (from *mestizo*, "mixed," or "hybrid"), with its informing cultural and value traits and orientations, especially its linguistic (that is, Spanish) contribution, are critical elements for our understanding of intergenerational issues. This first *mestizaje* defines or profiles many Hispanics — that is, mostly the first generation: those Hispanics who were here before the Mayflower, those later migrations to the U.S.A., and the more recent migrations of the 1980s from the Caribbean and Central and South America. This first *mestizaje* can be illustrated in noting the Puerto Rican reality. The *mestizaje* of the Puerto Rican is threefold: Spaniard, Amerindian, and African, while that of the Chicano or Mexican is mostly Spaniard and Amerindian. This is highlighted by Don Pedro Albizu Campos in his "Discurso del 'Dia de la Raza'" of October 12, 1933:

> That there is African blood, I too carry it in my veins and I carry it with the supreme pride of human dignity. We have here Indian blood . . . I too have Indian blood and because of that I feel perfectly American, indigenous American. . . . That there is white blood in us? I too carry it in my veins. . . . We are an historically predestined people,

because Puerto Rico is the first nation in the world where the unity of the spirit with the biological unity of the body takes form.[1]

Dating back to 1925, the Mexican philosopher and diplomat José Vasconcelos, in his seminal work, *La Raza Cósmica: La Misión de la Raza Iberoamericana,* emphasized this conceptualization of *mestizaje.* In recent years Virgilio Elizondo and others have popularized it and extended its meaning.

If we just noted the *first mestizaje,* we would be only presenting a partial picture of Hispanic American reality. For indeed the Hispanic American heritage of *mestizaje* is a double process that goes beyond the first encounter of Spaniard (European), Amerindian, and African. The second encounter involves the Anglo-American civilization and the Latin American. This *second mestizaje,* as we see it in the "new generation" Hispanic Americans or the second and third generation Hispanics, is the *double mestizaje* or bilingual/bicultural reality critically important for one's understanding of Hispanic North Americans. These "new generation" Hispanics are further defined by their English language dominance and North American cultural ethos.

Mestizaje is excellently summarized by Orlando Costas when he says:

This double *mestizaje* is the result of the military, cultural and religious invasions and conquest that have characterized the history of Hispanics in North America. Each has produced multiple variants. In the case of the first *mestizaje,* it produced the multiple national and regional cultures of the Latin American mosaic; in the case of the second, the emerging regional and subcultural varieties to be found in Hispanic communities through the U.S.[2]

Virgilio Elizondo, for whom *mestizaje* is a central theological category, notes well the ambivalent status of the *mestizo* (particularly the second *mestizaje*) in present North American society.

1. Pedro Albizu Campos, *La Conciencia Nacional Puertorriqueña* (Mexico, D.F.: Siglo Veintiuno, 1974), pp. 195-96.
2. Orlando Costas, "Hispanic Theology in North America," B.T.I., Liberation Theology Consultation, Andover Newton Theological School, October 25, 1986.

The *mestizo* does not fit conveniently into the analysis categories used by either parent group. The *mestizo* may understand them far better than they understand him or her. To be an insider-outsider, as is the *mestizo*, is to have closeness to and distance from both parent cultures.[3]

This cultural phenomenon of *mestizaje* produces what I call a "triple consciousness" in the "new generation" Hispanic or second and third generation Hispanic. Let me explain: W. E. B. Dubois, the great African-American thinker and writer, spoke about the "Double Consciousness" experienced by black persons in the U.S.A. They were part of the U.S.A.'s society (insider), yet were conscious that they were "outsiders" because of their color and existing racism. This psychosocial reality has had serious implications in the development of the African-American experience. In a similar way the "triple consciousness" of the second *mestizaje*, the second and third generation or "new generation" Hispanic, places them often in the role of being "insiders" and "outsiders" to the dominant Anglo-white group, but also "insider" and "outsider" to the first *mestizaje* group (first generation Hispanics) as well. They are "insiders" — totally accepted and affirmed — only among themselves (the second *mestizaje* group). The plight and psychosocial, not to say spiritual, condition of the second *mestizaje* in this "triple consciousness" is precarious.

The cultural phenomenon of *mestizaje* and its "double consciousness" (for first generation) and "triple consciousness" (second and third generation) greatly defines the matrix of intergenerational dynamics — a significant dynamic that can either unite or divide Hispanics.

Further defining our matrix is the social element of the setting of Hispanic American culture. In other words, the cultural phenomenon of *mestizaje* and its attendant "double and triple consciousness" takes place in a social context that by and large must be defined as *oppressive*. While there might be "pockets" of success (i.e., the Cuban "golden exile") highlighted by the media and others, and praised by such books as *Benjy López*, "the overwhelming majority of Hispanics have been condemned, along with the majority of [African Americans], to be the permanent underclass of North American society."[4]

3. Virgilio Elizondo, *Galilean Journey: The Mexican American Promise* (Maryknoll, N.Y.: Orbis, 1983), p. 18.

4. Orlando Costas, *Christ Outside the Gate* (Maryknoll, N.Y.: Orbis, 1989), p. 113.

An article in the *Boston Globe,* entitled "Census says good life still eludes most of U.S. Hispanic population," says in part:

> Large segments of the fast-growing Hispanic population are still poor, unemployed, uneducated and shut out of the best jobs, the Census Bureau reported yesterday.
>
> The 22.4 million US Hispanics made small steps out of poverty and unemployment and toward a better-educated population during the past decade.
>
> But when compared with that of the non-Hispanic population, the living conditions of Hispanics are grim: 21 percent of Hispanic children are poor, compared with 11 percent of all US children; and 26.6 percent of the total Hispanic population is poor, compared with 11.6 percent of non-Hispanics.
>
> As of 1990, only about half of the Hispanic population had completed high school. Hispanic workers tend to be concentrated in low-wage service jobs or as laborers, and their earnings trail those of non-Hispanics, despite slight gains between 1982, the end of the last recession, and 1989.
>
> "We see Hispanics making gains, but the question is: Are the gains sufficient? And the answer is almost always no," said Robert Paral, research associate at the National Association of Latino Elected and Appointed Officials. "We still see Hispanics overrepresented at the lower socioeconomic levels."[5]

Some of you may not wish to hear this truth. But we need to be deeply aware of it because it further defines the existing and potential irritants (if not conflict) between the first generation (first *mestizaje* group) and the second and third generation (second *mestizaje* group). For by and large the second *mestizaje* Hispanic group — because of its linguistic acquisition, meaning English dominance, and its value orientations, meaning assimilation of North American ethos — is "doing better" as far as socioeconomic factors are concerned.

This cultural/social reality is the first basic and fundamental element of the matrix defining intergenerational dynamics. We must un-

---

5. "Census Says Good Life Still Eludes Most of US Hispanic Population," *The Boston Globe,* April 11, 1991.

derstand the distinctive cultural and social phenomena affecting the first *mestizaje* group and the second *mestizaje* group. We must equally appreciate and affirm each of these *mestizaje* groups. Notwithstanding the historical reason for their genesis, the fact of the matter is that our Hispanic family includes both — thus we must learn from each. We must appropriate those positive lessons learned and values acquired in each group so as to enrich our one "Pueblo" — the Hispanic American.

Communication/Language

The second basic category or element of our matrix is *communication/language*. While under culture one can cover both linguistic and communication factors, I believe that this element must be identified separately because of its critical role in understanding intergenerational dynamics.

The Spanish language is the unmistakable contribution of Spanish culture to Hispanics. It is a "living language" which has been infused by the contributions and vitality of the Amerindian and African cultures. To the second and third generations the English language has been the unmistakable contribution of North American culture. As such, language has given Hispanic Americans not just a linguistic tool of communication, but a particular *Weltanschauung*. The science of anthropology, linguistics, and philosophy have documented well that language is indeed a mediating tool between human beings and their world. Ruben Alves states it well:

> We do not contemplate reality face to face. From the moment we are born, things do not come before us in all their nakedness; they come dressed in the names that some community has given them. The community has already defined how the world is, and hence it knows what the world is. This knowledge of the world is crystallized in language. . . . Language is always interpretation. In interpretation objects fuse with emotions, the world and the human being embrace. . . . Talk about the world, then, is always interpretation of the world.[6]

6. Ruben Alves, *Protestantism and Repression* (Maryknoll, N.Y.: Orbis, 1985), pp. 26-27.

To touch the language structure of a person is to touch the heart of his or her view of self and world. Language is thus important — to say the least!

The linguistic reality of Hispanic Americans, while predominantly Spanish, has in the second and third generations (the second *mestizaje*) increasingly become English dominant. Let me share with you some demographic data from the Census Bureau, somewhat dated, but yet indicative of a trend among Hispanics. Justo González in his study for the Fund for Theological Education, entitled *The Theological Education of Hispanics,* notes the following:

> Although . . . a high percentage of Hispanics are born in the United States, a very large percentage also report that Spanish is the language spoken at home . . . 75% of all Hispanics counted by the census, reported that Spanish is the language spoken at home . . . roughly one fourth of those who speak Spanish at home, or 19% of the Hispanic population, also declared that they do not speak English well, or that they do not speak it at all. There is no statistic regarding the use of Spanish by the 25% of Hispanics who declared that English is the language most used at home. It is likely that roughly half of these are bilingual, or have at least some use of Spanish. Thus, it would appear that the usage of language among Hispanics in the U.S. breaks down as follows:

English only	12.5%
Bilingual with English preference	12.5%
Bilingual with Spanish preference	56.0%
Spanish only	19.0%[7]

When you add some of these figures together, you come up with an interesting and significant communication scenario: (1) 68.5 percent of Hispanics are bilingual; (2) 81 percent of Hispanics understand English; and (3) 87.5 percent of Hispanics understand Spanish. Gonzalez concludes, and I concur, "Thus, *bilingualism* is likely to continue being a feature of the Hispanic community in the foreseeable future."[8]

7. Justo González, *The Theological Education of Hispanics* (New York: The Fund for Theological Education, 1988), pp. 11-12.
    8. Ibid., p. 12.

While it is true that "the cultural focus of Hispanic American identity is obviously the Spanish *language* and the culture associated with it,"[9] we must note carefully that those English-language dominant Hispanics (bilingual/bicultural second and third generation Hispanics) are bona fide and genuine Hispanic Americans. In our sons and daughters, language alone should not exclude from having a Hispanic identity.

I think we do well in listening to the warning noted by González when he stated,

> Among Hispanics, and specially among those whose sense of unity is most acute, there is heard a frequent warning: let us not so idolize our culture that we oppress another Hispanic who does not speak as we do, or even one who has never learned how to speak Spanish because the pressures of society were too great.[10]

Clearly the communication patterns set by our linguistic dominance or preference are critical elements defining the matrix of intergenerational dynamics.

The Church

The third basic category or element of our matrix is the church. To speak of the church element in our matrix means to focus on that institution that for many of us has been the central arena of intergenerational concerns. It is in the Hispanic church that many of us see more clearly the intergenerational dynamics of first *mestizaje* and second *mestizaje* Hispanics.

The Hispanic church, in its most active and socially significant expressions, has played for Hispanics the role of cultural survival. It has been for the first *mestizaje* group the locus of Hispanic cultural validation. Family values, language, music, art, customs, and symbols of the first *mestizaje* group (the first generation) have been sustained, nourished, and affirmed in the Hispanic church. When the dominant culture pressed for a forced assimilation, it has been in the enclaves of our Hispanic

9. Ibid., p. 32.
10. Ibid., p. 33.

churches that many have found their Hispanic culture and values safeguarded.

The Hispanic church at this time in history is at an impasse regarding the second *mestizaje* Hispanics. In many places it is ambivalent as to its mission, role, or status with second and third generation Hispanics (the second *mestizaje*). Will the Hispanic church provide the cultural and spiritual "space" for the second *mestizaje* Hispanics to find their bilingual/bicultural values affirmed? In the interest of preserving their Hispanic culture — which they have every right to do — will the Hispanic church also be oppressive to the second *mestizaje* Hispanics, also attempting a forced assimilation?

I am delighted to note that many Hispanic churches are awakening to a new understanding of their mission with their *own* — second *mestizaje* Hispanics. These churches are not rejecting their sons or daughters simply because they prefer potatoes, peas, and carrots to rice and beans or tamales — or simply prefer to speak English. I commend associations like H.A.B.B.M. (Hispanic Association for Bilingual Bicultural Ministries) and others which are emerging to respond to the great needs and contributions of the second *mestizaje* Hispanics.

Cultural/social reality, communication/language, and the church are three of the basic and fundamental elements of the matrix of intergenerational dynamics. They are the fundamental elements that define the context which forms and informs intergenerational reality. I believe to the degree that we come to grips with these elements, that is, understand the significant role they play in the lives of Hispanics, to that degree will our responses be relevant and substantial. I believe that the intergenerational issues that arise in the church will be properly confronted as we gain an in-depth knowledge of these elements.[11]

11. For a more detailed exploration of some of these basic elements, see Eldin Villafañe, *The Liberating Spirit: Toward an Hispanic American Pentecostal Social Ethic* (Grand Rapids: Eerdmans, 1993), esp. chap. 1, "Hispanic American Reality," and chap. 2, "Hispanic American Religious Dimension," section on "Social Role of the Hispanic Protestant Church."

AGENDA FOR THE 1990S: SPELLING OUT OUR PROJECT

In view of this brief survey of the matrix of intergenerational dynamics, let me suggest several "Agenda Items" for the Hispanic church in the 1990s. Some are quite simple and basic, yet we must, in many cases, remind ourselves of them.

1. Given the immigration trends from the Caribbean and from Central and South America, and the reality of present Hispanic Americans, we will have and need Spanish-speaking churches in the 1990s and beyond.

2. The social-cultural-spiritual needs of first *mestizaje* Hispanics need to be attended to and served. Thus, we must support those political and ecclesiastical policies that affirm and enhance the Spanish language and Hispanic culture.

3. By all demographic data, second *mestizaje* Hispanics are increasing in numbers and will represent an important economic and political force in the U.S.A.; thus we will need a special Christian leadership response by the church in terms of evangelism, discipleship, Christian education, worship, and liturgy as well as theological and ethical formulations.

4. The "double consciousness" of first *mestizaje* Hispanics and the "triple consciousness" of second *mestizaje* Hispanics must be addressed by a church that not only loves unconditionally but also provides the proper ethos for their distinct Hispanic psycho-social identity.

5. Notwithstanding the importance of the Spanish language, the Hispanic church must be inclusive in defining Hispanics, thus English-dominant Hispanics must be received as bona fide Hispanics. In other words, Spanish should not be the exclusive criterion for a Hispanic identity; and the Hispanic church, of all institutions of society, should be in the vanguard in defining and establishing this self-definition.

6. Given the socioeconomic conditions of most Hispanics in the U.S.A., the Hispanic church must develop a theology and social ethic that call for economic and political engagement.

7. Bilingual and bicultural issues, policies, and ministries will in-

creasingly define the Hispanic church in the 1990s. Only those churches that have vision and that prepare themselves to meet this new reality will reap a fruitful harvest for the Lord's kingdom.

▼ PART THREE ▼

URBAN THEOLOGICAL EDUCATION

Essential Elements for an Effective Seminary-Based Urban Theological Education Program

OUR CITIES — OUR NATION

Our cities are not what they were fifty years ago, twenty-five years ago, or even ten years ago. Our cities are multiethnic, multicultural, and increasingly multilingual. They are increasingly divided between the "haves" and "have-nots" and between people of color and white. While Marshall McLuhan spoke of a "global village" to highlight the critical communication and interdependency of contemporary life, we need to further qualify it to read an "*urban* global village." The apparent contradiction of urban/village underscores the reality of the global process of people/ethnic movements from village to major urban centers. This worldwide phenomenon is also (given our immigration patterns) the experience of large cities in the U.S.A. Be it Boston, New York, Philadelphia, or Los Angeles, they also are experiencing this globalization process: a multiethnic and multicultural reality is increasingly defining its ethos.

Ben Wattenberg, the author and demographer, speaks of our cities and our nation as experiencing "the dawning of the first universal nation." The notion of the United States as a "universal nation" is not new since historically the great American experiment has represented this very aspiration. It is important to note that this internal development is consistent with the external "global mission" of America found in its cultural narratives — stories that shape American images of self and world.[1]

While not all theological education must or can be done in or by the seminary, and while not all theological education done by the seminary is substantive or relevant to all contexts, constituencies, or confessions of faith, the implications both of demographic trends and American history for theological education are basic and simple. If we are to effectively educate leaders for our urban scene, this contextual reality — multicultural and socioeconomically poor — must inform all aspects of the theological enterprise. While urban ministry encompasses ministry to the middle class and wealthy in our cities, too, the predominant focus in most seminary-based urban theological education programs (a correct one in my judgment) is on ministry to the "inner cities" of our great metropolis. The specificity of educating for ministry with the "poor" has biblical warrants as well as sociocultural relevancy.

SIX ESSENTIAL ELEMENTS (SIX "C's")

Six categories will be used to present essential elements for an effective seminary-based urban theological education program. These elements can be used as criteria or as a basis for evaluating existing and projected models. The six essential elements or six "C's" are: constituency, contextualization, curriculum, community, coexistence with the host seminary, and cost.

Constituency

A basic and fundamental question that seminaries must raise as they train urban leaders is the question, *Whom* are we educating? There are several factors to this question of constituency. First to be addressed is the issue of the "clergy" vs. "people of God" paradigm.

---

1. Roger G. Betsworth, *Social Ethics: An Examination of American Moral Traditions* (Louisville, Ky.: Westminster/John Knox, 1990), pp. 107-37; see also "Toward the First Universal Nation," *The Boston Globe*, March 16, 1991, p. 22.

We live in a complex urban world. Its diversity and numerical growth, the limitations and breakdown of present delivery systems of human, ecological, and socioeconomic resources,[2] call for *all* God's children to exercise their God-given gifts (1 Cor. 12:7) for the Shalom of the city. We must train *all* of God's people for ministry. The church as a whole must be educated — lay as well as clergy — to respond effectively and faithfully to the challenges of urban ministry. The whole gospel must be witnessed to by word and deed by the whole church. Given the times and the context in which we live, the burden is on those clergy-teaching models to justify, or should we say to rationalize, their elitist-focused constituency.

Urban theological education should be structured to train both clergy and laypersons. While distinct tracks can be provided for each, the best programs will provide for interaction by way of a flexible curriculum. In other words, the curriculum will provide courses and projects where both the potential clergy and layperson participate jointly. This principle applies equally in my judgment to those programs that focus on existing clergy. The dynamic and rich interaction of persons and issues that is found in a local class setting where the "people of God" model is present is critical for the life and mission of the church in the city. With an increasingly older, second-career, part-time, or bivocational student body, both good economic stewardship and sound pedagogical principles call for transcending the clergy model to a "people of God" model of seminary education.[3]

The second factor in the constituency equation to be addressed is the "monoethnic" vs. multiethnic focus. The demographic changes in America, as reported by the U.S. Census Bureau for 1990, are momentous. The census shows that the proportion of whites in the population continues to decline. In the past decade the number of Asian Americans has more than doubled and the Hispanic population has grown more than 50 percent. According to Carl Haub, a demographer at the Population Reference Bureau, "cultural diversity probably accelerated more in the 1980's than any other decade." The *Boston Globe* article from

2. See J. John Palen, *The Urban World*, 3rd ed. (New York: McGraw-Hill, 1987); Clarence N. Stone, Robert K. Whelan, and William J. Murin, *Urban Policy and Politics in a Bureaucratic Age*, 2nd ed. (Englewood Cliffs, N.J.: Prentice-Hall, 1986).

3. Edward Farley, *Theologia* (Philadelphia: Fortress, 1983).

which this quote was taken states that, "Even compared with the period of high immigration early in this century, the 1980's will be seen as a period of remarkable ethnic change in this country."[4]

Our cities are the locus of this ethnic and cultural diversity. Our cities, already inhabited by the "traditional minorities" — African American, Hispanic, Asian, and Native American — are now receiving thousands upon thousands of new immigrants from Haiti, Brazil, the Caribbean, and Central and South America, as well as from Asia and the Pacific Islands. The emerging churches in American cities increasingly reflect this reality. In Boston, and I may add in other major cities in America, "these immigrant and poor-black churches could dominate organized religion in the city."[5]

The seminary of the future and the future of all seminaries depend on how well they respond to this ethnic and culture mosaic. Seminary-based urban theological education programs must be at the vanguard in providing creative and committed multiethnic and multicultural theological education. Programs must serve this diverse constituency as well as train other whites and traditional constituencies to minister with and in this new reality.

A third factor in the constituency equation is that of gender. Seminaries are becoming more sensitive to the needs and contributions of women. Yet, there is much room for improvement. In the case of urban theological education programs, the gender issue is paramount. Irrespective of the "ordination question" of women by many denominations, urban ministry in our cities would cease to exist if women were "left out." The role played by women in urban ministry is significant and historic. Be it Catherine Booth in London, Aimee MacPherson, "Mama Leo," Nellie Yarborough, or your local church missionary, our cities have been greatly impacted by the sacrificial witness and ministry of these women. Urban theological education programs must reflect at all levels the inclusion of women on a par with men. Administration, faculty, staff, and curriculum must reflect the gifts of the whole body of Christ. Space must be provided in our urban theological education

4. Barbara Vobejda, "Broad Growth Is Found in U.S. Hispanic, Asian Population," *The Boston Globe*, March 11, 1991, p. 4.

5. Maureen Dezell, "The Third Coming," *The Boston Phoenix*, June 22-28, 1990, p. 6.

programs in which a spirit of "Lifting Voices — Praising Gifts"[6] can reign.

Let me briefly note a final factor in the constituency equation. Our cities reflect diversity at many levels, including religious diversity. A Christian urban theological education program must emphasize and encourage an interdenominational presence. The many churches dotting our "barrios" from distinct Christian denominational confessions should find their students welcomed and affirmed in our programs.

Contextualization

Contextualization means many things to many people. The best image and clearest biblical insight into its meaning is the Incarnation. It is the "Holy Other" pitching God's tent among us in the person of Jesus Christ (John 1:14; Phil. 2:5-11). To contextualize our urban educational endeavors is to "pitch our tent," meaning the seminary resources — financial, intellectual, or personnel — in the context of urban ministry. It is to humbly express an "urban kenosis" — emptying oneself for the service of others. For the seminary, church, or school, this contextualization is excellently summarized by Dr. Robert Pazmiño as he underscores the significant questions raised about contextualization by the Third Mandate Programme of Theological Education Fund:

> What about *missiological contextualization?* Is the seminary or school focusing upon the urgent issues of renewal and reform in the church, and upon the vital issues of human development and justice in its particular situation? (A liberationist perspective would question the notion of reform and renewal in the face of injustice and would instead propose revolution and complete transformation.)
>
> What about *structural contextualization?* Is the church or school seeking to develop a form and structure appropriate to the specific needs of its culture in its peculiar social, economic, and political situation? (A liberationist perspective would require that the form or

6. March 1990 and March 1991 Center for Urban Ministerial Education (CUME) Women's Conference theme.

structure be liberating and transformational at points where the culture is oppressive.)

What about *theological contextualization?* Is the church or seminary seeking to do theology in a way appropriate and authentic to its situation? Does it seek to relate the gospel more directly to urgent issues of ministry and service in the world? Does it move out of its own milieu in its expression of the gospel?

Finally, what about *pedagogical contextualization?* Is the seminary or school seeking to develop theological training which attempts to understand the educational processes as a liberating and creative effort? Does it attempt to overcome the besetting dangers of elitism and authoritarianism in both the method and goals of its program to release the potential of a servant ministry? Is it sensitive to the widespread gap between the academic and the practical?[7]

In a practical sense let me summarize some of the implications of contextualization for a seminary-based urban theological education program.

1. Contextualization implies that the urban program is *situated* — both administratively and programmatically — in the context of ministry, the inner city. One does not do effective urban ministry at a distance.
2. Contextualization implies a commitment to the Shalom of the city. The city, as context of training and ministry, is looked upon as a positive locus of God's redemptive activity. A wholistic gospel is presented that emphasizes both evangelism and social justice in the seeking of the Shalom of the city (Jer. 29:7).[8]
3. Contextualization implies the application of the "homogeneous unit principle" in assuring that the directors, deans, or chief administrators of the urban program be representatives of the constituency served. In other words, urban programs should be led by African Americans, Hispanics, or others that have the credibility

---

7. Robert W. Pazmiño, *Foundational Issues in Christian Education: An Introduction in Evangelical Perspective* (Grand Rapids: Baker, 1988), pp. 158-59.

8. Eldin Villafañe, "The Jeremiah Paradigm for the City," *Christianity and Crisis* 52, nos. 16/17 (November 16, 1992).

and legitimation of the inner-city churches served. There are a significant number of white directors of urban theological education programs. Yet, given the multiethnic and multicultural reality of our inner cities, it would be wise to engage and develop indigenous leadership.

4. Contextualization implies that a significant number of the faculty are indigenous. An urban program needs a "critical mass" in terms of African-American, Hispanic, and other multiethnic teachers. All efforts should be placed in securing competent faculty members that are representative of the community served. This means that our seminaries must do more than they have done in recruiting and retaining minority faculty. Full faculty status and rank must be the goal of the seminary for its core urban faculty.

5. Contextualization implies that the staff as well as members of advisory boards and other policy committees reflect as much as possible the community served.

6. Contextualization implies the presence of liberating forms and structures in the educational delivery system. What this means is that the sociocultural reality and needs of the urban church and constituency inform the appropriate organizational and administrative style and ethos of the urban training program. For example: (a) overly hierarchical organization and administrative structures should be lessened; (b) bureaucratic and other "paper" formalities should be reduced; (c) face to face and personal contact should be the norm; (d) time of classes (evenings, late afternoons, weekends) should reflect the time the constituency have at their disposal, as many church leaders and students must work (during the day) to support their families, in addition to their church ministries; (e) location of classes — when possible, it is wise to decentralize the operations of urban training programs. In other words, class locations can be distributed in existing church and parachurch facilities throughout the city. This is not only good stewardship of finances and facilities, but also permits the urban training program an opportunity "to impact more than one specific community, preferring instead to be salt and light to the entire city."[9]

9. Bruce Jackson, "The Center for Urban Ministerial Education (CUME): Impact on Boston," unpublished report, Boston, Mass., 1990.

More will be said regarding theological and pedagogical contextualization when we address the other elements in our report.

Curriculum

To speak about curriculum is to speak about all the factors in a school or program that contribute to the fulfilling of the objectives of theological education. Good theological education, in general or urban, focuses on the following triple objectives: (1) to *form* pastors and teachers (and other leaders) among the people of God; (2) to *inform* them about the Scripture, tradition, reason, and experience in social, cultural, and concrete historical contexts; so that (3) they may serve as agents of *transformation* in the churches, denominations, and social communities in which God has placed them.[10]

More specifically, the purpose of urban theological education should include the following:

1. To develop an appreciation and understanding of the complexities and pluralities of the city and of the diverse ministries of the urban churches and parachurch organizations.
2. To foster theological reflection and the integration of theological studies with the practice of ministry in urban contexts through supervised ministry and course work while contributing to personal growth, spiritual development, and vocational identity.
3. To meet specific needs of differing constituencies:
   (a) to help students with urban backgrounds integrate past urban experiences and to develop appropriate strategies for ministry;
   (b) to help students from non-urban backgrounds by providing new urban experiences as a basis for learning and developing appropriate strategies for ministry; and
   (c) to provide education that meets the special concerns of racial and ethnic minority students.
4. To develop skills in ministering in a variety of settings in the urban situation:

10. "New Alternatives for Theological Education," *Fraternidad Teológica Latino-americana*, Quito, Ecuador, 1985, mimeographed, p. 9.

(a) among the poor and disadvantaged;
(b) among the city's diverse constituencies: blacks, Hispanics, Asians, Haitians, Portuguese-speaking, and others;
(c) among working-class groups;
(d) among professionals and "high-risers" (gentrification); and
(e) among various denominations and faith communities.[11]

In the case of urban church leaders already engaged in meaningful ministry, one can further add the following development objectives: (1) developing greater competence in ministry; (2) developing greater self-understanding (identity) and sense of mission (vocation); (3) developing coherence between explicit theology and implicit practice; and (4) developing their leadership potential in the church and the greater society.[12]

As Robert Pazmiño reminds us, "Curriculum is the vehicle or medium through which educational vision takes roots."[13] If we are to seriously impact our cities and educate competent and compassionate leaders, our curriculum must go beyond the "classical disciplines" to develop action-reflection approaches as epistemologically sound and socially relevant.

In an action-reflection model of curriculum and teaching methodology, theory does not take the place of practice — nor practice the place of theory. There is a constant dialectic that permits courses to combine "field" experience — the whole city, churches, community, and other institutions — with classroom and library/research activities. This speaks of a *pedagogical contextualization* that is informed by the biblical paradigm of leadership education, an action-reflection approach (i.e., Samuel and the school of the prophets, Christ and the disciples, and Paul at the school of Tyrannus [Acts 19]).

In each of these biblical paradigms there is both action and reflection in the training process. Each phase informs the other, thus enriching the learning experience. We do well in contemporary Christian edu-

11. "Purpose Sub-Committee Report: Theological Education in and for an Urban Global Village," unpublished report in The Center for Urban Ministerial Education: Evaluation and Long Range Planning Project, Boston, Mass., 1987.
12. Ibid.
13. Pazmiño, *Foundational Issues*, p. 207.

cational circles to exhaust — exegetically or otherwise — the meaning and implications of these biblical models before we copy the "world" model of leadership education.

Excellence in an urban theological education program — especially its curriculum — is not defined by the university/seminary "guild," with its heavy emphasis on theoretical content mastery. Rather, *excellence* will be contextually defined by the quality, yes, rigorous demand, of integrating theory and practice in courses — in the overall curriculum. Make no mistake, academic or theoretical knowledge (of the classical disciplines) is important. Yet, sound educational philosophy and the biblical paradigms challenge us to go beyond to a wholistic understanding of learning, leadership education, that gives serious weight to the dialectic of practice.[14]

It is important to note that an action-reflection approach in curricula design also permits for the development of *theological contextualization*. Theology, as well as the other disciplines, is informed by the context of ministry. "Doing theology" becomes a normative experience of the student in this approach.

Justo González, in referring to several models utilizing the action-reflection approach, makes the following pertinent remarks:

> This is a model which believes that theological education must not only be grounded in the place where a Christian is already ministering, but should also make use of that ministry and that experience as part of the raw material for theological reflection. While it believes in academic rigor, it also believes that such rigor is not an end in itself, but is rather to be placed at the service of education, and that there are therefore other considerations that are just as important.[15]

Let me briefly note some specific programmatic elements that a sound urban theological education curriculum should have. They will

14. See, among others, Donald Schön, *The Reflective Practitioner: How Professionals Think in Action* (New York: Basic Books, 1983); Don S. Browning, *A Fundamental Practical Theology* (Minneapolis: Fortress, 1991); and Paulo Freire, *The Pedagogy of the Oppressed* (New York: Seabury, 1970).

15. Justo González, *The Theological Education of Hispanics* (New York: The Fund for Theological Education, 1988), p. 102.

be spelled out in four basic categories: (1) curriculum divisions or tracks; (2) courses; (3) mentored ministry/colloquia program; and (4) other program features.

(1) *Curriculum divisions or tracks* notes the diversity of the student body and their educational goals. As I noted previously, it is good to have all students in a class session — thus providing rich interaction and feedback. Yet, many of the students have distinct goals for studying and many find themselves at different levels of "city experience" and academic accomplishments. Good curriculum design will provide courses and experiences for the "urban novice" as well as for the mature city leader. Distinct educational achievement tracks with proper recognition should be established. In other words, the curriculum should provide for certificates, diplomas, or other such recognition of completion for those who may be interested in attending one or several course sessions or series of seminars, as well as a more programmatic and extended diploma track. By the same token, a more extensive track should be developed for those interested in a seminary degree — M.A., M.Div., and even D. Min. and Ph.D.

Given the reality of many urban church leaders — which includes many pastors — alternative degree tracks should be developed. Individuals without a college degree should be given the opportunity to do undergraduate and/or graduate degree programs. Various creative programs already exist which are providing these services.[16]

(2) *Courses* should cohere with the educational mission and objectives of the urban theological education program. These can range from the basic "classical traditions" — Bible, theology — to a more contextual one (i.e., The City in the Bible; Urban Theology and Ministry; Inner-City Ministry; Urban Issues; History and Theology of the African-American Church; Introduction to Community Organizing; Hispanic Theology and Ministry; Racism and the Church). When at all possible, a committee composed of students (who may be urban leaders), faculty, and administration should design the year-to-year curriculum. This will not only respond to the changes and transformation

16. For distinct and creative models see, among others, those provided by New York Theological Seminary, the Center for Urban Theological Studies, Fuller Theological Seminary, and Gordon-Conwell Theological Seminary's Center for Urban Ministerial Education (CUME).

occurring in the city — its churches, its people — but will protect against "morphological fundamentalism." This term is used to refer to "the fact that certain forms or structures may take on the character of being sacred and, therefore, exempt from question or examination."[17] Ministry in the city, given its oft-changing scenario, requires constant evaluation and mid-course adjustments. Curriculum, to be relevant and effective, needs to be cognizant of this reality.

In view of the ever-increasing multilingual reality of our inner cities, it is important that urban programs reach out in distinct languages to the constituency in context. That means that given the large Hispanic reality in our cities, the question is not just of servicing them, but in doing so in their own language — Spanish. This can be also said, depending on the ethnic presence in a particular city, of courses taught in French (for Haitians) or Portuguese.

While there are many courses one can suggest that make up a good urban curriculum (like the examples I noted above), let me highlight three which I think are critical: (a) Leadership in Ministry; (b) Research and Writing in Urban Theological Studies; and (c) The Church and the Community: Urban Structures and Municipal Delivery Systems. These courses can be taught under whatever name seems proper for the program, but what is important is the emphasis on certain knowledge or competency.

Leadership in Ministry responds to the individual student's questions on personal identity and vocation. It deals with the substance and style of the urban church leader, while providing the knowledge and skill to develop other leaders in the students' church or ministry.

Research and Writing in Urban Theological Studies is an attempt not only to upgrade students' writing and research skills, but also to teach practical principles for lifelong learning.

The Church and the Community: Urban Structures and Municipal Delivery Systems seeks to introduce and develop a knowledge of city institutions and the church's role. It not only provides for development of referral files on distinct municipal services, but also should give exposure to and knowledge of the complex city systems. This course provides an opportunity to emphasize the social responsibility of the church and the need to confront the injustices and systemic evil of contemporary society.

17. Pazmiño, *Foundational Issues*, p. 216.

(3) *Mentored Ministry/Colloquia Program* acknowledges that classroom learning must be enhanced by an intentional and intense exposure to dialogue, counsel, and serious reflection on the student's personal identity and vocational development. Reflection groups that seek to integrate classroom content, church-ministry experience, and personal spiritual formation are one way of addressing our concern here. Several schools and programs have found it necessary to structure a more formal program variously called "colloquia" or "mentored ministry" that throughout the student's seminary life seeks to be a bridge from classroom learning to the reality of ministry. The credit-bearing nature of these programs is important. It notes that this element of the curriculum is not peripheral but central to solid urban theological education.

(4) *Other program features* notes that sound urban theological education must creatively seek to respond to emerging needs and opportunities in the city with programmatic elements that may be of short or long duration: the development of church/ministry sites for student assignments must be constantly updated and evaluated; special short-term seminars or courses for particular churches or denominations should be offered; seminar forums or guest lecture series provide opportunity to bring in experts from distinct disciplines; church-based economic leadership programs can be developed to respond to the pressing needs of the city; citywide conferences and consultations, involving both local and national leaders, provide opportunity for addressing specific church and urban issues (e.g., women's ministry, Christian development, urban theology and ministry). These conferences are not only an important source of information, but they also serve to identify and inspire urban leadership.

Community

No seminary-based urban theological education program will succeed without having the "blessing" or credibility of its host community. The leadership of the urban program, as well as its teachers, must be respected and trusted. It is imperative that the seminary establish a good relationship with key leadership of the constituency to be served before the urban program begins. This principle should also reign when introducing new programmatic (i.e., new language tracks) elements to the urban program. As early as possible, urban leaders should be involved at all levels of program development.

While seminary-based urban theological education programs have their own legal boards, all efforts should be made to develop an urban advisory board composed of community leaders. The seminary should seek to have urban leaders represented in the school's legal board. The advisory board can serve in many ways to facilitate communication between the community-neighborhood, the urban theological education program, and the host seminary. Members of the advisory board can also serve the urban program by being members of admissions, finance, and curriculum committees.

The sense of ownership of the urban program by the community is enhanced by the advisory board and committee membership of urban leaders. The leadership of the urban education program should not only live in the context of ministry, along with other program staff and teachers, but should also exercise their gifts in the churches and community. Strong community networks should develop between the urban program and the community. The resources — facilities, intellectual, personnel — of the urban program should increasingly be placed at the disposal of the community — be it church, parachurch, or community social agency.

Ownership of the program by the community is a slow and sensitive process. No one formula will do it. Yet, the overall ethos of "servant-leadership" practice by the urban program leaders, staff, and teachers will go a long way. The "whole" of the elements discussed in this report (i.e., constituency, contextualization, curriculum, etc.), as a *gestalt*, provide that vehicle which enables the community to have a sense of ownership.

It is important that a newsletter/bulletin be developed by the urban theological education program. It will provide an opportunity for better communication of urban educational events, as well as for communicating student-churches' activities to the whole community.

The urban program should develop a good relationship with other urban programs in the community. These other programs might include non-ATS schools servicing Hispanic, African-American, or other constituencies in the city. Opportunities should be explored to interface, dialogue, or enter into joint projects with these schools given the reality of their ministry in the same context, often the same constituency, and, of course, serving the same Lord. In many cases, these non-ATS schools can be "feeders" to the urban theological education program for students desiring further education. The urban program can often be, like the case in Boston (CUME), the advanced training ground for many Bible Institute teachers and directors.

The circle of "community relations" should be enlarged by the urban theological education program to include other national urban programs. Biblical stewardship and practical realities call for a sharing of educational as well as resource (funding) leveraging "technologies and skills" among urban theological educational institutions.

Coexistence with Host Seminary

The distinct structures and interfacing/relationship patterns, roles, and styles that develop between the host seminary and the urban theological education program are critical to the success of urban ministry. While there may be different organizational-structural ties (models) expressed as program, center, or campus, certain guidelines can be noted that apply across all of these and that are important for successful and faithful urban theological education ministry.

First, seminary involvement in urban theological education ministry must be clearly understood by all as part and parcel of the seminary's mission statement. The urban program is not peripheral to the life and mission of the seminary but a central part of its mission. Neither demographics, financial need, the "in thing," or expediency motivates involvement, but a clear call to service.

Second, seminary involvement in urban theological education should be long-range. Urban programs should not be viewed or planned as a three- or five-year pilot project. One does not "experiment" with urban ministry; rather, after prayerful discernment (yes, study too), the seminary moves, as the Lord leads, into partnership with the urban church.

Third, seminary involvement in urban theological education means a serious commitment and stewardship of resources — financial, intellectual, personnel, and so forth — for the urban program. It is important, though, that the urban church demonstrate its partnership by increasingly sharing its limited resources (2 Cor. 8:2-5).

The seminary's appointment of the director of the urban theological education program is one of the most critical elements toward the success of the urban program. Much prayer and dialogue with the urban church leadership should take place before such an appointment.

(1) The director's academic credentials should be on a par with the host seminary's requirement for faculty/administrators. Given the nature of seminary life, it is important that the director have full faculty status and rank and that he/she be perceived as a "peer" by the rest of the faculty.

(2) The director must have credibility with the urban church constituency. As noted previously, preferably that person will be an ethnic urban leader.

(3) Among the qualifications, the director needs to:

(a) Allow his/her colleagues to work as partners, enabling a strong sense of mutual ownership to develop; (b) be able to evoke trust from among a widely diverse group of persons in terms of ethnicity, denominational and theological backgrounds; (c) be versatile, able to feel at home and function comfortably in a wide variety of religious communities; (d) take authority lightly and yet know where the buck stops; (e) be concerned for the personal growth and nurture of all staff members; and (f) be stimulated by living on the frontier of theological education, willing to run the risk of new ventures and able to respond to new options and ideas.[18]

The seminary must not marginalize the urban theological education program by keeping it at a distance from their normal calendar of activities. In other words, the urban program will be institutionalized as much as possible, without compromising its urban integrity, to the host seminary:

(1) The director, as part of the faculty, will serve the host seminary, as time permits, on committees, will speak in chapel, and will fulfill

18. George and Helen Webber, *The Center for Urban Ministerial Education — An Evaluation 1986-87: Contextualized Urban Theological Education* (Boston, Mass: Gordon-Conwell Theological Seminary, 1987).

other functions that will encourage his or her full acceptance by faculty, administration, staff, and students.

(2) The seminary will provide space and promote urban chapel services, seminars, urban guest speakers, and other functions that will "in-house" the urban vision to the whole seminary community.

(3) The seminary will provide an office space for the urban program on its campus. This will provide visibility to the program as well as a practical location to interact with campus students and faculty.

(4) The seminary will keep their "community-at-large" (trustee, administration, faculty, staff, students, alumni, donors, friends) informed through their normal communication channels of the "events" of the urban program. From time to time special communications highlighting the urban program will be called forth.

(5) The seminary will treat the urban theological education program budget as a central piece of the overall school budget, not just as a peripheral project. (More will be said in the next section on cost.)

(6) The seminary will encourage qualified faculty to teach in the urban program. Teaching in the urban program will fulfill part of the normal teaching load for faculty. There will be an effort to monitor other seminary teaching programs (i.e., Continuing Education) so that they do not compete with faculty serving the urban program.

(7) The seminary, by word and deed, will encourage all of its departments and units to be open and disposed to provide their services to the urban program.

(8) The director of the urban theological education program should be a member of the president's "Administrative Council" or similar high-level seminary-wide administrative committee.

The urban program, and by implication the director, should be under the supervision of the seminary's academic vice president or academic dean. Given the nature and complexity of the urban scene, and the need for sensitive and timely handling of many issues and needs, it is critical that the urban program be organizationally "housed" at the highest rung of authority. It should not be subsumed under second- or third-level authority structures of the seminary (i.e., director of continuing education, director of extension education, associate dean, etc.).

The seminary's academic dean and urban program director will schedule systematic meetings throughout the academic year. Communication lines should be open and flexible. The staff meeting minutes of the urban program should be sent to the academic dean, as well as to other pertinent seminary administrators or committees. A semester progress report and a final academic year report by the director should be submitted to the dean of the seminary.

The president, academic dean, and other key administrators of the seminary need to make their presence felt in the urban program. Besides attending graduation functions and other special events in the city, it would be good if during the year official meetings would be scheduled with the urban director and staff on site.

The seminary's trustees should not only be kept informed of the urban theological education program through normal communication channels, but every effort should be made by the president to "bring them down" to the city. This is very important, particularly for those trustees not familiar with urban life. A two- or three-year plan should be instituted that will see to it that all trustees have had an opportunity to visit the city — participating in the urban theological education program at one level or another.

The seminary will welcome and encourage the urban program's advisory board, urban church leaders, and students to visit and participate in seminary functions and events.

Cost

A sure indication of a seminary's commitment to urban ministry is its *financial* investment. Long-range urban theological education programs can be costly. It is imperative that the seminary be financially committed for the long haul. The urban budget should be a central part of the host seminary's overall budget allocations. All means should be explored to place the urban ministry budget on a solid financial base — it should not be supported by "soft monies." Endowments, long-range foundational support commitments, and trustee prioritization should be sought.

At the beginning of the urban theological education program, the seminary should demonstrate its financial commitment by presenting a three- to five-year funding program. This financial plan will show the seminary's obligation to fund the urban program at a level that does not depend on "outside" funding sources for it to get off the ground and succeed. Relative to the seminary, this "dependency factor" from outside sources — urban churches, foundation giving, and so forth — can range up to 50 percent of the total cost. In subsequent years a scale-down of seminary investment in the urban program can be planned. This is contingent on a serious financial development program instituted for the urban program that will see increased revenues. As part of the urban program, a development officer or portfolio (in the director's job description, perhaps?) should be in place. Whether responsibility lies with the director, another staff member, or other seminary officials, the funding officer should work closely with urban program staff in all facets of proposal and/or funding program development.

A word about personnel salaries is perhaps appropriate here. If we want excellence in our urban theological education program, we must "pay" excellent salaries. Often salaries of urban program staff are so meager that turnover is frequent. Retention requires a just salary scale, one that reflects the professional qualifications of staff and real expenses of city living.

In view of the socioeconomic status of the inner-city churches, it must be understood that they will not be able to carry the major financial burden of urban theological education programs at first. As previously noted, though, all means must be explored for the constituency served to exercise their biblical stewardship by supporting the urban program (2 Cor. 8:2-5). Besides tuition and fees, other cost recovery and financial development projects can be developed by the urban churches. Among the activities that can be included are: (a) a special urban theological education day at each of the schools' participating urban churches; (b) a special banquet for scholarship and programmatic support; (c) inclusion of the urban theological education program in the urban churches' list of missionary giving; (d) from time to time a special request letter for gifts by the churches; (e) a special committee of "friends" of the urban program that includes community-wide representation of business persons and others committed to giving and developing financial support for the program; and (f) the development by urban program students, with staff support if possible, of "creative entrepreneurship projects" — from school T-shirts and buttons to gospel music concerts.

The seminary must earnestly seek a true partnership with the urban churches, foundations, and the Lord's people everywhere in developing sound fiscal responsibility for its urban theological education program.

CONCLUDING REMARKS

As we approach the twenty-first century, the challenges of urban living and ministry will increase exponentially. The church of the Lord Jesus Christ must prepare a leadership *willing* and *able* to confront the challenge.

The conditions of our cities, the call of our Lord, and the commitment of the Lord's people all point to a greater challenge for urban theological education programs to contribute to the Shalom of the city. This challenge is a challenge to excellence and faithfulness . . . one that needs biblical wisdom and Spirit guidance.

> Seek the Peace of the City . . .
> Pray unto the Lord for it:
> For in the Peace thereof shall
> Ye have Peace.
>
> (Jer. 29:7)

CHAPTER 9

Theological Education in the Urban Context

DOUGLAS HALL

Urban training needs to come from the interests and long-term needs of urban people. It should model what it teaches, first of all, by not being just another event that uses the city, but rather is used by the city and its people for their own spiritual and social needs and purposes. It is too easy for an educational institution to feel that it should have an urban training program and proceed to put one together. The temptation is to want to talk intelligently about the topic, rather than to perform the tasks that amount to doing biblical Christianity in the city. Urban training needs to be a part of the answer, not a part of the problem. Otherwise the complexity of the urban environment could render our efforts not only nonproductive but even counterproductive. And if our efforts are counterproductive over the long run, the question can honestly be asked, "Whose side are we on?"

A THEOLOGY THAT SEES THE CITY AS A STRATEGIC ENVIRONMENT FOR CHRISTIAN MINISTRY

The city and its people have an infinite array of needs, and ministry must address these needs relevantly, but to do so it must see the environment first of all as a strategic one for ministry, and not simply as needs.

The strategy of the apostle Paul was to impact the city, and many of the letters of the New Testament reflect this focus by bearing the names of ancient cities. The message of the gospel was to begin in the capital city of a subservient Hebrew nation and spread to its entire region and then to the world (Acts 1:8). Help was requested by the poor saints of Jerusalem, but the clear strategy of mission in the first century was not merely to help the city. Simply sending help can become a very paternal, nondevelopmental approach, and such approaches help only initially and in geographically limited ways. The city networks almost everything that is in it, for good or for evil. Social problems such as drugs and family breakup, once associated with inner cities, are problems everywhere today. When the spiritual and social needs of people in cities are met, we will have already begun to meet the future needs of people living in the suburbs. As churches die in cities they eventually begin to die in concentric rings around cities.

When we see these realities and become concerned for our posterity and our region over the long run, we must be concerned to train people to take the city very seriously. Our Christian future demands that we train them as best we can, under God, to perform as productively as possible for the kingdom of God. We cannot thus simply be training people to hold things together in a dying church, but we must be training them to build existing churches and plant new ones. The social ministry of the church must be at its most mature level in cities. By "mature" I mean existing in very healthy indigenous church and parachurch systems, and meeting needs in a way that also develops existing communities. When we begin to do this in cities, we will know how to do it anywhere; in fact, we will almost automatically do it in the nonurban areas, most of which are affected by cities. Paul followed his missionary vision of Macedonia by going directly to its capital city of Philippi (Acts 16:9-12).

REALITIES EXPERIENCED IN THE URBAN ENVIRONMENT

Students of the city must be prepared spiritually and psychologically, socially and strategically, to minister in an area that is complex, heterogeneous, dynamic, and manipulative.

1. *Urban complexity requires that pastors be trained in the basics of sociocultural systems, and that they fit into a ministry that seeks to be effective over the long run.*

a. *Training in the basics.* Cities have their political and dynamic delivery systems that are both complex and numerous. A seminary training program must inform students about these areas, but can only begin to touch the surface. Students must be trained in how to research their environment and have tools so they can use its systems, but a seminary does not have the luxury to train extensively in these areas. The program I am involved in, though stressing the above concerns, is based on a social analysis theory that focuses on conceptual constructs basic to all social environments. For example, we teach how to research and carry on social and spiritual ministry in (1) primary systems — that is, systems that meet needs via the relational networks of family, extended family, ethnic community, and the natural interrelationships found in more intimate neighborhood communities; and (2) secondary systems, which meet needs via organizational and economic types of interaction. The job often involves building the former systems up and making the latter systems operate justly. The poor normally function better in primary systems than in the secondary systems. The most vital forms of Christianity often exist among the poor in many cities. Therefore ministry to the poor is vital from the social justice perspective, and from the perspective of strategy as well.

b. *Gearing our ministry to the long-term concerns.* Jay Forrester, in his book *Urban Dynamics,* tells us that "change in a complex system commonly causes short-term responses in the opposite direction from the long-term effect" (page 112). Thus, if we are to accomplish goals that have long-term effects, long-term involvement is often a prerequisite, or at least having involvements which have good follow-up systems. I often tell my students, "If it falls apart after you leave, it does not show how important you were, but how unimportant." Sometimes our own need to be needed can contribute to a very negative result in the city. Self-centered involvements do not belong in urban ministry.

2. *Urban heterogeneity requires that cross-cultural training be a central concern in all legitimate urban training programs.* It is all too possible

for people who are even well-trained in cross-cultural concerns in over-seas situations to operate inappropriately in urban efforts in this regard. Cognitive knowledge must be followed up by supervised experiences, and even then some people more naturally have this gift than do others. An absolute need is that those who plan to minister to another culture must positively care about those people, be able to have effective com-munication with them, and understand how they perceive their own needs before even attempting to think about relevant ministry to them.

3. *Cities are dynamic; therefore training programs must develop the stu-dent's ability to do analysis before applying learned methods.* Eighty per-cent of a particular population of a city can change in two years, and this is only one of many changing urban dynamics. Methods that work in one part of a city at one time will not necessarily work there two years later (motion pictures of events and buildings in neighborhood areas may seem like ancient history shown even three years later). We, therefore, cannot be heavy on teaching a lot of specific methods and techniques. Future ministers need to be taught how to analyze com-munities and their situations regularly. Problems often need to be an-ticipated because relevant ministry often has a significant tooling-up period, and the need for what you are planning may be over by the time you are ready to do something. Or the need may have become too critical by that time to have any basic effect on causal factors. Not all cities are changing rapidly, but all cities are changing.

4. *City populations often feel very manipulated by many dynamics in their environments,* such as the dynamic of change just mentioned. The poor, particularly, are manipulated and thus are very leery of new plans de-signed to benefit them. In this regard indigenously developed programs are by far the best. Even the designing of an urban training program for the city by a seminary will itself often be seen as a threat to that urban area; cooperation will be very slow in coming from urban people. Therefore, the best and most long-term urban training programs are those that have been asked for and developed by urban people who work with a seminary to design these programs, and the seminary responds by training and assisting those who want to do the job, rather than by initiating or mobilizing the city for the seminary's agenda.

REALITIES OF THE WORKING ENVIRONMENT IN AND THROUGH WHICH THE URBAN PRACTITIONER MINISTERS

1. *The person who ministers needs to be analyzed in an urban training program.* Burn-out is very common, and often is due to personality and family factors apart from the actual environmental pressures. We encourage spouses to attend classes because marital disunity can be one of the major factors in failure in urban ministry. A personal analysis is always done by students and reviewed by friends, supervisor, and faculty in the program in which I am involved. Our program requires a major paper on urban ministry where the salient aspects of an urban ministry are looked at from a student's perspective. We teach experimentation on paper rather than experimentation on people. These papers are often very practical tools for both evaluation and ministry planning.

2. *The organization through which ministry is performed needs to be looked at by those who plan to do urban ministry.* The limitations and assets of particular organizations, denominations, and churches need to be known. This is often overlooked by those who have idealized notions regarding ministry in the city. Understanding these working structures has a lot to do with setting proper expectations for the practitioner. This is a major concern in setting up a long-term ministry involvement designed to make significant contributions to the kingdom of God in the urban environment.

3. *The community and its analysis is central to relevant ministry in an urban context.* This topic was the most frequently mentioned by past students now in urban ministry as needing to be focused on in any urban ministry training. It is almost impossible to conceive how long-term church growth can occur in a typical urban neighborhood without continual and relevant interaction with the people and structures of the major contextualized community. This must be taught in such a way that the information is gathered and processed via both data and personal involvement interactions. A training program needs to enable students to make use of this information in their ministry development. Parachurch involvement needs people who can do a program and analyze data to tell them what to be doing to prepare for future ministry.

4. *Showing the importance of an ongoing study of models of ministry is critical in urban training.* Most enduring and creatively successful urban programs involve themselves in the study of ministry models in either a formal or informal manner. There are many methods utilized in studying models, but the stress often needs to be on what can easily be done by a practitioner later on in ministry. The dynamics of ministry do not often afford the time to do extremely detailed studies, and thus this is far too important an exercise to be done only in the classroom and not in the field.

A STRATEGIC THEOLOGY OF TRAINING DESIGNED FOR COMPLEX ENVIRONMENTS

The experience of Lent has much to teach us about the dynamics of urban training. Our Lord, according to John 1, came into an environment that seemed opposed to his involvement, or at best did not understand him or his purpose. "The light shines in the darkness but the darkness has not understood it." The early events of Mark's Gospel, in the first three chapters, describe a counterproductive process, and it all is prefixed by "the beginning of the gospel about Jesus Christ, the Son of God."

Cities are often not receptive places for the development of Christianity, and those who would minister there will often have a Lenten experience in their ministry. In my own training I spend a lot of time initially bursting bubbles and showing how the complex environment of a city can work counterproductively despite our very best intentions. Our students need to be brought to the point of crying out: "You keep showing us what won't work. Well, is there anything that does?" At that point in the learning process, students are ready to be taught about urban ministry. Our training too often focuses only on learning and not enough on the humbling experience of unlearning. Generally speaking, we are not naturally prepared to do urban ministry. An urban training program must teach unlearning. It must prepare us for the difficult. Salvation comes to us personally when we face the reality of our sin and limitations, and cry out to our Lord for his mercy and help. There is productive ministry on the other side of the cross, but a part of us has been left in front of the cross, and we now go forward not as persons totally competent in ourselves. We have not simply been trained; we have been discipled.

CHAPTER 10

Paul, Leadership, and the
Hispanic Church

EFRAIN AGOSTO

M any of us who are Hispanic professionals in ministry, in addition to our ministries of pastoring, preaching, and teaching, would lay claim also to a larger ministry. We seek to provide opportunity to those who, for reasons of social status, economic level, race, or gender, are kept out of the mainstream of access to jobs, housing, and education. A theological statement of these efforts might be called the ministry of helping all people to realize all of their God-given potential. Certainly in the Latino community of the United States there is an important advocacy role for the church in this area of ministry.

Moreover, there are different dimensions to this role of providing opportunity. It is not just about opening doors; it is also about providing the proper training, about empowerment for making best use of those doors. For example, if we as a Latino church work toward opening the doors of the best North American universities to our young Hispanic students, we ought also to ensure that such education is utilized for the service of our community and our church. Hispanic leadership development that is faith-based needs to be about empowerment of both laity and ministry for leadership in our church and its larger community. Young Latino leaders should prepare in the professions. But their business, legal, educational skills, and, yes, theological training as well should be employed for the betterment of the Latino community, and not just for personal gain.

Those who have worked long and hard in the ministry and other professions have this access and empowerment motif as a vocational goal. My purpose here is to reflect on some biblical paradigms for such a ministry orientation. Sociological questioning, now a growing discipline in biblical studies, will help us determine what Paul believed about access, opportunity, and leadership development in his churches.[1]

PAUL AS AN URBAN MISSION STRATEGIST

Recently, scholars like Wayne Meeks, in his book *The First Urban Christians,* have investigated in depth the sociological impact of urbanization on Pauline church development. But Meeks was not the first. In a classic study, *Missionary Methods: St. Paul's or Ours?* (1912), Roland Allen, a missionary to China, reminded a generation gone by about Paul's church-planting strategies. While not a sociological study per se, Allen's emphasis on the locus of Paul's missionary work, the city, instructs our search for models of church leadership development in the Hispanic community.

Allen describes how Paul set out to "evangelize provinces" in Asia Minor and Europe by establishing "centres of Christian life in two or three important places from which the knowledge might spread into the country round."[2]

Invariably these "centres of life" were the important cities of the Roman Empire. They were places like Lystra and Derbe, key Roman military posts and centers of government administration. They assured the access needed to spread the gospel into other areas of that Roman province of Galatia.

It was in these urban centers of the Roman provinces, rather than the provincial towns of the countryside, that Greek civilization and education also continued to flourish. As Allen says, "Everywhere, Roman

1. There is a wide body of literature in this area. A fairly thorough bibliography of studies in New Testament social analysis can be found in Daniel Harrington, "Second Testament Exegesis and the Social Sciences: A Bibliography," *Biblical Theology Bulletin* 18 (1988): 77-85. For an excellent descriptive overview from an evangelical perspective, see Derek Tidball, *The Social Context of the New Testament: A Sociological Analysis* (Grand Rapids: Zondervan, 1984).

2. Roland Allen, *Missionary Methods: St. Paul's or Ours?* (repr., Grand Rapids: Eerdmans, 1962), p. 12.

government went hand in hand with Greek education."[3] It was this Greek education that provided Paul with the means to communicate the gospel. The Scriptures Paul utilized to prove his message were not translated into the provincial dialects, but into the cultured Greek of Alexandria (where the Septuagint — the Greek Old Testament — was produced three hundred years earlier). Moreover, Paul utilized the language of the *polis* (the city) to preach, teach, and write.

Thus the influence of Greek culture, which continued to be most evident in the cities of the Roman Empire, also served well the Christian mission. Greek language education was centered in the city, where it could be most influential. Allen affirms that "it was to places where that education was established that St. Paul naturally turned."[4] This was done in order to facilitate the spread of the gospel message.

The places where Paul turned to establish and develop churches and their leaders were also centers of commerce. These cities were, as Allen says, "foremost in every movement of policy or thought."[5] And thus they were leaders from among the cities and towns of the provinces. This is an important factor because when a city and its people see itself, and also those outside the city see it, as having a "life larger than its own," it becomes a focal point for unity and responsibility before the outside world. People will turn to it for the latest trends and ideas. The Christian mission had to have a place in such centers if its message was to be heard and promulgated.

We must note here the current-day demographic realities that most Hispanics in the United States live in the great urban areas of the country. Historian Justo Gonzalez makes this point abundantly clear:

> The majority of the Hispanic population is urban. In 1980, 50% of all Hispanics lived in central cities, with an additional 37% living in metropolitan areas outside the central cities for a total of 87% urban dwellers. Since it is likely that most of the undocumented Hispanics who were missed by the census are living in large cities, that percentage is probably higher.[6]

3. Ibid., p. 14.
4. Ibid.
5. Ibid., p. 15.
6. Justo Gonzalez, *The Theological Education of Hispanics* (New York: The Fund for Theological Education, 1988), p. 11.

Early indications from the 1990 census are that Hispanics are now spread to even more urban areas across the country. The large presence of Latinos in the cities of the U.S. has some important implications if we are to take Wayne Meeks's sociological analysis and Roland Allen's missiological study of the apostle Paul's urban ministry approach seriously. Leadership development of the Latino community and its churches can go a long way toward promoting the impact of Christianity on the cities and, as we learn from the Pauline strategy, on the whole world.

STRATEGIC URBAN CENTERS

In Paul's day, the cities whose names comprise the titles of our New Testament Pauline letters were places through which the whole world passed. The commercial and intellectual wealth of the world was exchanged here. Because of the great roads that passed through them, the entire Roman Empire was accessible from these urban centers. Thus the strategy was clear: The Christian church had to be established in the cities if the whole world was going to hear the gospel message.

Once this strategy was put into practice by Paul and his associates, the apostolic mission was greatly enhanced. In a relatively short period of time, perhaps less than a decade (c. 48-57 C.E.), so much had been accomplished that Paul could write to the Roman church in c. 57: "from Jerusalem and as far round as Illyricum I have fully preached the gospel of Christ," and further, "since I no longer have any room for work in these regions . . . I hope to see you in passing as I go to Spain" (Rom. 15:19, 23-24, RSV).

Had Paul preached in every village and small town of these Roman provinces? In less than ten years? Hardly, but he left a strong Christian presence in such key cities as Philippi, Thessalonica, Corinth, Ephesus, Colossae, and the important border cities of southern Galatia. What Paul had done in spreading the gospel so quickly and thoroughly in the East was only to plant small cells of Christians in scattered households in some of the strategically located cities of the northeast Mediterranean basin. Paul's follow-up strategy was to strengthen these churches by means of letters and personal visits by himself and his co-workers. But most significant for our purposes, Paul sought to encourage potential leaders from among these churches to establish new groups of believers in the nearby provincial towns and villages. Thus Paul's urban mission strategy functioned as a leadership development strategy as well.

Leadership Development in the Pauline Churches

How did Paul develop leaders and why? What relationship was there between what Paul did and what was expected in the larger Graeco-Roman society? Our biblical study around these issues will help us draw out some implications for leadership development in the Hispanic Christian community today.

We will begin by exploring Paul's teachings about leadership. This we must do provisionally since Paul does not set out to establish any kind of "theology of leadership." Rather we must ascertain as best we can something of Paul's thought around this area as we study such statements as those related to his call to ministry, his exhortations to imitation of himself, the issue of suffering in the ministry, and his discussions of spiritual gifts.

Theological Basis of Pauline Leadership Development: Access

Paul believed leadership in the Christian church depended solely upon divine initiative — the call to ministry. This was the case in his own life. We learn, for example, from Galatians 1 and 2 that Paul's appeal to the Galatians concerning the authority of his apostolate is that his call to leadership does not come from human agency but the divine initiative (Gal. 1:1) in calling Paul to take the gospel to the Gentiles: "He who had set me apart before I was born, and had called me through his grace, was pleased to reveal his Son to me, in order that I might preach him among the Gentiles" (Gal. 1:15-16, RSV).

Since Paul's call was dependent on God's prerogative rather than human sufficiency, would that not be the case for others as well? It seems that way when we look at one of Paul's responses to the problem of party strife in the Corinthian church:

What then is Apollos? What is Paul? Servants through whom you believed, as the Lord assigned to each. I planted, Apollos watered, but God gave the growth. So neither he who plants nor he who waters is anything, but only God who gives the growth. (1 Cor. 3:5-7, RSV)

In this text, Paul argues that all leaders and workers in God's field are dependent on God for their call and their ultimate effectiveness. Because God takes the initiative, there is an equality of call ("as the Lord assigned to each"), an equality of function ("the one who plants and the one who waters are equal" — v. 8a), and an equality of reward ("each shall receive his wages according to his labor"). There is no indication elsewhere in Paul that these principles did not apply across the board in all his churches (although concrete practice may vary from church to church). Paul appears to affirm that church leadership is available to people from all walks of life because ultimately it is God's decision to call and appoint. Just as Paul received his apostolic call from divine initiative, he seems to have believed that all Christian workers would have that basis for their call to service. The leader is a leader because he or she responds to God's call regardless of personal social status. Because of that, the church need not reflect the elitist structures of the outside world in its practice of leadership.

This empowering approach to leadership is further exemplified by a key text for our discussion, 1 Corinthians 1:26-31, excerpted here:

For consider your call, [brothers and sisters]; not many of you were wise according to worldly standards, not many were powerful, not many were of noble birth; but God chose what is foolish in the world to shame the wise, God chose what is weak in the world to shame the strong, God chose what is low and despised in the world, even things that are not, to bring to nothing things that are, so that no human being might boast in the presence of God.

Gerd Theissen, among others, has argued for a sociological understanding of the categories presented in this text.[7] Paul has educational,

7. Gerd Theissen, "Social Stratification in the Corinthian Community," in *The Social Setting of Pauline Christianity: Essays on Corinth* (Philadelphia: Fortress, 1982).

political, and familial divisions in mind. The Corinthian church consists of a majority of people who are not philosophical sages, politically connected, or well-born nobility. To these, the church affords the opportunity, unlike the outside world, to function in leadership and thus "bring to nothing" those standards that seem important ("things that are") outside the church.

"Become Imitators of Me"

Imitation language is another way that Paul seeks to convey open opportunity. The texts are well known: 1 Thessalonians 1:6; 2:14; Philippians 3:17; 1 Corinthians 4:16; 11:1. The pattern is similar: "Become imitators of me"; the vocabulary is almost exclusively Pauline. When Paul calls for a response to his authority in these texts, it is couched in the language of "do as I do" (imitation) rather than in the language of "command — obey." John Schutz puts it this way: "Because Paul's life as an apostle itself reflects the power of God made manifest in the gospel, the apostle becomes a 'norm' for Christians much as the gospel is a norm for apostolic behavior."

Moreover, Schutz goes on to argue that Paul is not the only one to be imitated. In 1 Thessalonians 2:14, the Christians there have become "imitators of the churches of God in Judea." Thus "imitiation for Paul is not a matter of disciples following a master."[8] Rather, because of the power of the gospel, Christian living and Christian leading are available to everyone who will listen, learn, live, and lead.

Indeed, Paul believed that the gospel is sufficient and leadership possible even in the face of human weakness. Thus,

> it is no accident that Paul counsels the imitation of himself. His whole apostolic self-understanding is shot through with this awareness of his personal service in weakness which is at the same time God's power in him. Such a relationship to the gospel is not reserved for the apostle alone.[9]

8. John Schutz, *Paul and the Anatomy of Apostolic Authority* (Cambridge: Cambridge Univ. Press, 1975), p. 226.
9. Ibid., p. 231.

All who wish to be of service in the Christian community should "imitate" Paul in his dependency on God's power for carrying out the task of leadership. Weakness and suffering are therefore an integral part of the imitation passages cited above. The Thessalonians became imitators of Paul and the Lord when they "received the word in much affliction . . ." (1 Thess. 1:6). The Corinthians are urged to imitate Paul (1 Cor. 4:16), but it is a Paul who as an apostle has "become a spectacle to the world" (4:13). Weakness and rejection are the signs of Pauline apostolate. Yet herein lies the key to God's power being exhibited. Weakness becomes power, and what Paul "urges is that the Corinthians become powerful through this same weakness. This is what they are to imitate."[10]

Power in Weakness

This apparent paradox in Pauline ministerial theology, "power in weakness," thus becomes still another basis for the empowering of leadership in Pauline congregations. More specifically, Paul's emphasis on the humiliating figure of a "crucified messiah" as a sign of God's power serves to open up leadership opportunities to even "the lowly of this world" as we saw in 1 Corinthians 1:26-31. To return to that text for a moment, we noted that according to 1 Corinthians 1:26 not many of Paul's followers in Corinth were "wise," "powerful," or "well-born" (i.e., born of the richest and noblest families in Corinth). For these individuals of lower strata to be organized into a religious group, that is, the Christian *ecclesia,* whose organizing symbol was the cross of Christ, something very meaningful and powerful had taken place in their lives: "[The cross] gave them access to an alternative source of power based upon an ideology which taught that the first would be last and the last first, that he who suffered most gained most, that the 'weak' had precedence over the 'strong.'"[11]

Paul used this paradoxical theology of power in weakness as a rallying point for community formation and leadership development.

10. Ibid., p. 229.
11. S. Barton, "Paul and the Cross: A Sociological Approach," *Theology* 85, no. 703 (1982): 15.

Leadership structures and values that existed in the larger society were inverted. Paul's teaching about a crucified messiah "turned upside-down notions of honour and shame, both those of the Romans (based on quest for personal prestige) and those of the Jews (based on Torah observance)."[12]

Worldly Leadership

However, Paul did not just have to deal with the leadership values of those outside the church. In 2 Corinthians 10–13 in particular, we find Paul counteracting leadership criteria developed within this church out of a *teologia gloria* rather than a *teologia crucis*. Once again we see Paul arguing that his authority as a leader comes from the Lord and this is the way it would be for all church leaders. "For it is not the one who commends himself [or herself] that is accepted, but the one whom the Lord commends" (2 Cor. 10:18). In this section Paul is apparently confronting the presence in the Corinthian church of a group of leaders (whom Paul calls "super-apostles," 11:5) who are espousing more popular criteria for leadership legitimacy, such as rhetorical polish and acceptance of remuneration. For Paul these are insufficient criteria for church leadership because they are based on human sufficiency and therefore result in human glory.

For Paul, those criteria that support the spread of the gospel are what counts, and if these include inglorious means, such as being willing to confront beatings, imprisonments, and "far greater labors" (11:23), then so be it. Paul and all Christian leaders can "boast" ("glory") in these because they all point to the great theological truth — God's grace is sufficient. God's power is made complete even in human weakness. The "weak" of the world can become the instruments of God's grace, the proclaimers of God's gospel, the leaders of God's church.

Paul's treatment of the problem of the "super-apostles" in 2 Corinthians further demonstrates his criteria for who can exercise leadership and authority in Christian congregations. Apparently, some of the Corinthian Christians fell prey to worldly standards of leadership such as rhetorical style and remuneration principles. Paul's theology,

12. Ibid.

the gospel, called for "supra-earthly" status dimensions, based on divine criteria. These dimensions inverted the normal standards of leadership, whereby those whose experience was one of suffering and lowliness in the world (such as Paul himself had experienced since becoming an apostle) were now candidates for ministry on behalf of God's gospel. Thus, while the criteria for exercising leadership become more difficult — that is, being willing to experience difficulty and rejection — they are nonetheless liberating and empowering because such leadership is available to folks who never before had such opportunities.

Charismata for Service

Moreover, when we speak about "empowering" we are reminded of one final aspect of Paul's criteria for leadership in the church: the "charismata." Paul's most fully developed statement about the gifts of the Spirit is found in 1 Corinthians 12–14 (cf. Rom. 12:6-8). Such scholars as Bengt Holmberg[13] have pointed out that in this important Pauline passage, the apostle does not set out to establish some kind of church order or "offices." Rather, argues Holmberg, Paul wishes to show that any Christian can be "enabled by God to practice . . . any gift, task or service of benefit to the whole church."[14] Even though the spiritual gifts are personal endowments ("To *each* is given the manifestation of the Spirit . . . who apportions to each one *individually* as he wills," 1 Cor. 12:7a, 11), the goal is for the entire community to benefit ("for the common good," 12:7b).

Moreover, the spiritual gifts give individuals a role within a given social structure, the church. With a role comes a sense of identity, thus empowerment. Those who might not have a significant role or function in the larger society now have a recognized role and identity in a particular community within that society — the Christian church. Leadership is thereby developed by the recognition of endowment by the Spirit of God, who is available to "each one."

Furthermore, since charismatic gifts are validated only insofar as

13. Bengt Holmberg, *Paul and Power: The Structure of Authority in the Primitive Church as Reflected in the Pauline Epistles* (Philadelphia: Fortress, 1978).
14. Ibid., p. 121.

they render service to the community of believers as a whole, the bearers and practitioners of the gifts have the opportunity to develop as leaders within the church as they learn to edify the church, not just the self. This leadership development principle is exemplified by the way Paul handles the gift of tongues in Corinth:

> For one who speaks in tongues edifies himself, but the one who prophesies edifies the church. Now I want you all to speak in tongues, but even more to prophesy. One who prophesies is greater than one who speaks in tongues, unless someone interprets, so that the church may be edified. (1 Cor. 14:4-5)

Becoming "greater" in the church is a matter of learning to do what is best to build up the church as a whole. And that is a basic principle of Pauline leadership. Indeed, the spiritually endowed individual, whom we might call a "charismatic leader," knows that his or her responsibility is to "build up the church." He or she does this with the guidance of the principle of love (1 Corinthians 13). Moreover, "ultimately, all are responsible and obedient to the same thing: the gospel; for the same purpose: service to the church."[15]

Once again Paul establishes divine initiative and spiritual endowment by God for a selfless purpose — service to the community. Worldly, human-based standards to carry out tasks tend to be self-inflating, argues Paul, rather than service rendering. The latter is what leadership in the church is all about.

Thus we have come full circle in our presentation. The ultimate authority on which Paul bases his leadership status in the church (and, for that matter, in the world) is the divine call to spread the gospel message. Since that message and that call depend upon divine initiative and divine empowerment, others too are free to respond and partake of leadership in this endeavor, regardless of social status. There is no guarantee of freedom from suffering in this calling. Indeed, actual suffering and perceived weakness become the *modus operandi* of leadership in the Christian movement.

This is why the acceptable definitions and criteria for leadership in the Graeco-Roman society are upended by the Christian gospel and

15. Ibid., p. 258.

are a source of confusion for some in Christian communities like those of the Corinthian church. Those who are willing to suffer, be undermined, and work with little earthly reward such as prestige, power, or prosperity of means become those whom the gospel calls the "wise" and the "strong" in God's new covenant community. The cross is the symbol of sacrificial leadership, but also the assurance of free access for all. Leaders in the Christian community are freely endowed with the gifts necessary for service, but these are to be exercised in community, and not for personal gain and fame.

THE PRACTICE OF LEADERSHIP DEVELOPMENT
IN PAUL'S CHURCHES

Who actually were the leaders in Paul's churches? Certain studies have gone to great lengths to provide a "catalog" of names and titles of those individuals associated with Paul's ministry.[16] We will not repeat these here, but concentrate on the social status of Paul's leaders and thus test out what we have perceived to be a Pauline "theology of access."

Meeks, for one, believes that the catalog of Paul's leaders points to a group that was essentially of higher social-economic status. How does Meeks arrive at such a conclusion? When we read about Paul's associates in such texts as Romans 16 and 1 Corinthians, we find such people as Phoebe, a "deacon" and "helper" (Rom. 16:1-2). The terms applied to Phoebe point to a woman who "has been the protector or patroness of many Christians, including [Paul] himself." Moreover, we can infer that she "is an independent woman . . . who has some wealth and is also one of the leaders of the Christian group in the harbor town of Cenchrae."[17]

The next two people mentioned in the Romans 16 passage are

16. The most well known of these studies is E. Earle Ellis, "Paul and His Co-Workers," *New Testament Studies* 17 (1971): 437-52; cf. also Holmberg, *Paul and Power,* pp. 57-67; Wayne Meeks, *The First Urban Christians* (New Haven: Yale Univ. Press, 1983), pp. 51-73.

17. Meeks, *First Urban Christians,* p. 60. The Greek term for "helper" *(prostasis)* can also refer to someone in a position of leadership, someone who "resides," not just who helps (cf. 1 Thess. 5:12).

Prisca and Aquila, who are called "fellow-workers" by Paul. They apparently owned a home big enough to house a church meeting (Rom. 16:3; 1 Cor. 16:19). They are mentioned elsewhere in the Pauline correspondence and in Acts (18:1-3). They are quite mobile; we see them in Rome, Ephesus, and Corinth. This fact, and the fact that they establish good-sized households in each city, indicates some modicum of wealth. As Ronald Hock has pointed out in his study on "tent-making," not all craftspeople such as Prisca and Aquila were small-time, low-pay laborers.[18] They could have been independent artisan types that did quite well for themselves.

What Meeks, Hock, Holmberg, and others point to in their analyses of Paul's leaders is that Paul's "mission strategy" must have influenced the development of a certain type of leader in his churches. Holmberg argues that Paul needed "energetic and influential people" to ensure the establishment and continuing growth of his churches.[19] Moreover, this effort would be best carried out by persons with "a certain kind of wealth and social standing: owning a house which can accommodate the church for worship, time and leisure to take care of the needs of others and financial means to do so, civil rights in one's city."[20] Such criteria point to a leadership class that emerges from higher social standing in the larger world. This runs counter to what we perceived as Paul's "open" theology of leadership opportunity.

Yet this is not the final word on the people who were actually leaders in Paul's churches. First of all, as Meeks is quick to point out, we must be cautious when dealing with the written data because it might mention only the most prominent of individuals, leaving out an entire group of individuals from different social classes who might have exercised significant leadership roles as well. Among these might be charismatically endowed leadership: leaders of worship, teachers, prophets — many of whom may or may not have been from upper levels of society. Such leaders are virtually excluded from mention by name in the Pauline letters, as well as in the New Testament as a whole.

18. Ronald Hock, *The Social Context of Paul's Ministry: Tentmaking and Apostleship* (Philadelphia: Fortress, 1980).

19. Holmberg, *Paul and Power*, p. 106.

20. Ibid., pp. 101-2.

Status Inconsistency

Second, simply because someone may seem to have a certain amount of wealth does not mean that they are the accepted leaders of the outside society. Meeks alerts us to the sociological phenomenon of "status inconsistency." Ancient society, because of its strict, hierarchical structures,[21] seems to have promoted the ambivalence of status inconsistency, in which an individual might meet the criterion for high status in one category but not in others. Thus, for example, in Corinth individuals "may enjoy a high rank in [such] dimensions . . . as wealth, identification with Latin elements in the colony, support by dependents and clients, and in one or two cases, civil office, but they may be ranked lower in others, such as origin, occupation or sex."[22] Such persons may therefore share values with higher social levels, but may not enjoy ready acceptance. They are not well integrated into the larger society and seek to change that. The Christian movement, with its open access to leadership, may well have been appealing to them.

The facts are that Paul does bring together several different social levels, including slaves, freed artisans, and "patrons" with homes large enough to hold church meetings. Even within these categories there may have been several divergent rankings. There are former slaves — freed persons — with advancement in terms of wealth and position, but without the corresponding acceptance by the larger society, largely because of their past and their relatively new status. There were apparently wealthy, independent women attached to the Christian movement (e.g., Lydia, Acts 17; Phoebe, Romans 16). They no doubt experienced tremendous resentment and rejection in the male-dominated society of the Graeco-Roman world. In the Pauline church, there was the opportunity apparently for these persons to exercise leadership gifts.

In addition there were wealthy Jews (e.g., Barnabas, Acts 5:36-37), whose religious stance was not well received in pagan circles, and Gentile proselytes to Judaism (e.g., Jason, Acts 17:1-9), whose adherence to the synagogue rather than to the pagan temple created dissonance for them

21. For an outstanding description of social class and order in Graeco-Roman society during New Testament times, see Ramsey MacMullen, *Roman Social Relations: 50 B.C. to A.D. 284* (New Haven: Yale Univ. Press, 1974).

22. Meeks, *First Urban Christians*, p. 70.

in relation to their community and neighbors. All of these conflicts, ambiguities, and contradictions are characteristic of status inconsistency and may have been additional motivating factors in the movement toward the Christian church by people with certain means, but not opportunities. Individuals who could not exercise their natural leadership skills in the larger society were now able to do so in the Christian community.

Thus our research into Paul's leadership theology is intact, though modified, when we look at Paul's practice of leadership. In fact, the Pauline churches did not automatically reflect the social structures of the larger society in terms of who becomes a leader. True, homeowners, independently wealthy people, and the like seem to be mentioned as Paul's associates more often than not. Nonetheless, this does not mean that they are the only leaders of the church. Moreover, even these are the "rejected" in terms of leadership in the world, and thus have an opportunity, access, not otherwise afforded. "Social outcasts," to use another appropriate term, do exercise leadership in the Christian community. Paul's theology is put into practice.

Perhaps the best example of "status inconsistency" in Paul's churches is seen in the role of women. The evidence points to female heads of households, owners of businesses, independently wealthy, travelers with their own slaves (Chloe, 1 Corinthians 1), and converts to Christianity without consent of their husbands (1 Cor. 7:13). Women also exercise charismatic functions in prayer and prophecy (1 Cor. 11:2-16) and are Paul's co-workers in teaching and evangelism (e.g., Priscilla and Aquila with Apollos, Acts 18:24-28). All of this points to individuals who both in terms of their position in the larger society and in terms of their participation in the Christian communities were breaking the normal expectations for women's roles. They were truly putting into practice Paul's theology of access, empowerment, and opportunity in church leadership.

IMPLICATIONS FOR THE HISPANIC COMMUNITY IN NORTH AMERICA

Do these findings in our biblical, theological, and sociological study of Paul, his letters, and his churches teach us anything about the plight of

Latinos in the United States, with particular reference to the Latino church?

Rudolf Bultmann, not often quoted positively in evangelical circles, nonetheless made a cogent point for our purposes when he wrote:

> Are we to read the Bible only as an historical document in order to reconstruct an epoch of past history for which the Bible serves as a "source"? Or is it more than a source? I think our interest is really to hear what the Bible has to say for our actual present, to hear what is the truth about our life and about our soul.[23]

I am convinced that a study of Pauline patterns of leadership development in his churches can speak to leadership development in the growing Hispanic community of the United States. A historical reconstruction of how leaders were chosen and developed in the urban congregations Paul established shows that the call and exercise of leadership in the Christian community were available to all who were willing to respond, work, learn, and even suffer.

That much is the same for Hispanic leadership in the Latino church of the United States. For the most part, leadership has emerged from the grassroots. It has not followed the criteria for ministerial leadership established by the North American church (i.e., university and seminary training, which in a sociological sense means becoming "middle class," an experience outside that of most Hispanics in this country).[24] Eldin Villafañe, in his book *The Liberating Spirit: Toward an Hispanic American Pentecostal Social Ethic,* has outlined well for us the history of sacrificial — and "uncredentialed" — leadership in the Hispanic Pentecostal church in this century.[25] Moreover, Villafañe con-

---

23. Rudolf Bultmann, quoted in C. Rowland and M. Corner, *Liberating Exegesis: The Challenge of Liberation Theology to Biblical Studies* (Philadelphia: Westminster, 1989), p. 72.

24. "Census Says Good Life Still Eludes Most of U.S. Hispanic Population," *Boston Globe,* April 11, 1991. The article notes that 25 percent of all Hispanics are considered poor in comparison to 11.6 percent of all non-Hispanics. "Poor" is defined in terms of the so-called poverty line.

25. Eldin Villafañe, *The Liberating Spirit: Toward an Hispanic American Pentecostal Social Ethic* (Grand Rapids: Eerdmans, 1993), pp. 89-102.

cludes that both the Hispanic Pentecostal church and the Hispanic Protestant church as a whole have been a "seedbed for community leaders," both ministerial and lay. It is because there are few other options available to the Latino community that the Hispanic church has developed as a place where "the emerging leadership in the Hispanic community . . . has been nurtured."[26] Villafañe further argues that "few institutions in society provide Hispanics the inter-personal and political skills that are nurtured in the minority church."[27]

HISPANIC EGALITARIAN LEADERSHIP

It is the position of this essay that there are biblical precedents for recognizing and celebrating this fact. The Hispanic church has always been the place to create and produce the leaders, not only for its church, but also for its community. The natural and open development of leaders that the apostle Paul taught and practiced has been the "rule of thumb" for the Latino church in its history here. Moreover, when Villafañe writes about the "egalitarian theology" that is characteristic of the Hispanic Pentecostal church in particular, he is echoing what we saw in Paul's development of "charismatically endowed" leadership in 1 Corinthians 12–14: "Because of the leveling of the Glossolalic experience, all can receive a 'word' from the Lord; 'calling,' ministry, leadership as well as theology is not just the province of an elite."[28]

Our argument is that this is not just the experience of Hispanic Pentecostals. It was in fact how the early church exhibited its enormous early growth: indigenous leadership development in urban churches without the limiting criteria of an elitist, hierarchical society. When the church began to limit the exercise of leadership to those in the upper echelons of society, or least began to lend more weight and authority to "rich Christians" simply because of their prosperity or position in society, the result proved detrimental.

Justo González, in a fascinating study on faith and wealth in the

26. Ibid., p. 107.
27. Ibid.
28. Ibid., p. 132.

early church, describes the phenomenon of aristocrats buying their way
into the ministry after Constantine's Christian conversion early in the
fourth century A.D.

> Since joining the ranks of the clergy was one of the few ways in which
> the *curiales* (the minor aristocracy of provincial towns) could avoid
> the heavy burden of their [tax] responsibilities, ordination became a
> commodity that some were willing to buy and others to sell. John
> Chrysostom complained about the priesthood being up for sale.[29]

In an earlier section, González cites L. W. Countrymen's study, *The
Rich Christian in the Church of the Early Empire*. Countrymen "analyzes
the conflict that arose between clergy and rich Christians who hoped to
have in the church the same status that their pagan counterparts enjoyed
in the clubs and societies of the time."[30] González cites this as a fourth-
century phenomenon. Earlier than that, "the roles of benefactor and
leader were kept separate" in the church. We see this in Paul's efforts in
leadership theology and practice, even though we can cite Corinth as one
example where conflicts existed between high status types and freedom of
leadership opportunity in church work. By necessity, if not by prescribed
theology, the Hispanic church in the United States has been one where
leadership has emerged without reference to status in the larger society.
This historical fact must be recognized, celebrated, and studied so that we
might glean important lessons about ongoing leadership development for
the Latino church and the church at large. What aspects of Pauline
leadership development and Hispanic church leadership development are
vital for the church in the 1990s and beyond?

New Challenges

The times are changing. The growth of the Latino population in the
United States means an increase in the complexity of our needs and

---

29. Justo González, *Faith and Wealth: A History of Early Christian Ideas on the
Origin, Significance, and Use of Money* (San Francisco: Harper & Row, 1990), p. 154.
30. Ibid., p. 134, n. 3.

problems. Therefore, there is a need for clergy more formally trained to confront these complexities. Moreover, while we have always produced our leaders, they have never had the voice and the power in the larger church structures, let alone in society at large. A larger and more complex populace will increasingly demand greater voice and opportunity in the existing denominational, ecclesiastical, and secular political institutions. This opportunity should be based on justice, leadership, and representational policies and not on whether we have the right degrees from the right schools. But experience shows that credentials still open doors even, sad to say, in the church world.

Thus we are back where we started at the outset of this article. The ministry of providing access and opportunity is necessary in the struggle for justice in the Latino church and community. We want and need more secular colleges and professions. We want and need more Latino seminary students and faculty. Leadership for our communities is not defined by these institutions and the credentialing process they represent. However, in order to service and represent our communities better in the years to come, we will need to either create our own such institutions or impact change on existing ones. A combination of these options is most likely what needs to happen.

In fact, the institutions (colleges, seminaries, graduate schools, as well as denominations) that identify and develop our ecclesial and community leadership can learn much from the Latino experience in grassroots leadership development. Thus the challenge to provide more opportunity for our up-and-coming Latino leaders works both ways. The traditional institutions of leadership development provide their resources and expertise to the community's leaders. The latter in turn remind the institutions of the biblical notions of leadership development. Divine calling, open opportunity, and faithful, sacrificial service are the criteria for church leadership, not management of narrow, hierarchical structures, unwieldy credentialing processes, and an elitist status.

Conclusion

We have tried to show that for the purpose of leadership development in the Hispanic community, the Pauline principle applies: "For as many of you as were baptized into Christ have put on Christ. There is neither Jew nor Greek, there is neither slave nor free, there is neither male nor female; for you are all one in Christ Jesus" (Gal. 3:27-28).

The apostle Paul believed that not only "putting on Christ" is available to all, but that leadership in the Christian church is available to all regardless of socioeconomic background. This Pauline principle of leadership development, which becomes a cornerstone of his mission strategy, must be applied to the development of the Hispanic church in the United States, its leaders, and, indeed, to its community as a whole.

▼   CHAPTER 11   ▼

Urban Theological Education for Church Leadership

BRUCE W. JACKSON

Several months ago I had a conversation with a colleague about the Center for Urban Ministerial Education (CUME). As we were talking, he stopped me and remarked, "CUME is really doing *ministerial education* as opposed to *theological education*." I prodded him on the difference and he explained that theological education was more conceptual, more theoretically oriented, while ministerial education was concerned about the practice, the "hands-on stuff," of ministry. I listened politely, but deep down something inside of me said that this distinction was missing the whole point. It was only a few months later, after reading some articles on the history and development of theological education, that I was able to label his distinction: It was the classic theory-practice debate that has plagued theological education for at least forty years.

Far too often, I fear, most theological educators would lump education for urban church leadership into the practical aspect of ministry. I would argue that we need to think of a new paradigm altogether, one that rightly places theory in proper perspective with practice. Rather than attempting to name such a paradigm, however, I would like to describe four aspects that should characterize any program providing theological education for urban church leadership. They are: (1) contextualization; (2) praxis-focused ministry; (3) grounded in the present, looking to the future; and (4) servant leadership. My experience since 1981 at the Center for Urban Ministerial Education will provide illustrations for these elements. Additionally, much of my discussion is focused through the lens of what seminaries are (or are not) doing in our major urban centers.

CONTEXTUALIZATION

Any urban theological education program worth its salt must be contextualized. What do I mean by this? The theological background of contextualization is related to the continual need for the gospel to enter into the time and situation (the context, if you will) of a particular people. Robert Pazmiño defines this as a process whereby God's truth and justice are applied to, and emerge from, concrete historical situations.[1] Thus, for instance, the forms of church worship will look and sound and feel different in various parts of the world. A culture that exists in an economically impoverished area, or one that is oppressed, will do its theologizing ("God and us talk") differently than a rich or oppressing society. What this means is that Christianity is continually challenged to make the truth of the gospel relevant to a society in a particular time, location, and historic condition. It is not that the truth of the gospel undergoes change, but rather the forms and the manner in which it is adapted to "fit" a culture.

Theological educational programs must also be contextualized.[2] A contextualized program of theological education concerns itself with more than communication of the gospel. It also considers the process by which one does theological reflection, the methods used in the program, the teacher, the course content, and the final purpose for the entire educational enterprise. Contextualization takes the issues and concerns of the constituents as its starting point for theological discourse. The process of theologizing ("doing" theology) begins from this starting point. Thus,

---

1. Robert Pazmiño, *Foundational Issues in Christian Education: An Introduction in Evangelical Perspective* (Grand Rapids: Baker, 1988), p. 55.

2. See, e.g., Max L. Stackhouse, *Apologia: Contextualization, Globalization, and Mission in Theological Education* (Grand Rapids: Eerdmans, 1988); Eldin Villafañe, "Essential Elements for an Effective Seminary-Based Urban Theological Education Program," chap. 8 herein.

truth is not derived in the abstract or in a "top-down" fashion, but by wrestling with the issues of the people. It is seen through the lens of our culture and society, which shapes how we view life. Yet it is based upon the revelation of Scripture. A basic way in which this is done is simply by acknowledging that the study of theology is not limited to Eurocentric thinkers. There are a variety of voices contributing to the theological enterprise. Afrocentric, Hispanic, Haitian, Brazilian, deaf, feminist, and other perspectives have contributions to make to the process of theologizing. Though some may not be comfortable with the answers these strands may formulate, their questions at least become part of the milieu.

CUME's Contextualization

Practically speaking, how does CUME contextualize itself as a program? One way is by implicitly asking the question, "How does the context (situation) and culture of ethnic groups impact all the elements of the theological educational ministry of the church?" CUME's attempt to contextualize its programs is seen in a number of ways.

Location

Most obvious is CUME's location. Its classes and administration take place in the city. Urban ministry is not done at a distance. After almost fourteen years of renting office space, Gordon-Conwell Theological Seminary purchased and renovated an old Victorian house which is now the administrative center of CUME's ministry. This commitment to purchase property is a tangible demonstration that CUME is here to stay. It is an incarnational presence, akin to what is found in Jeremiah 29:5, where the exiles were instructed to build houses and plant gardens.

Contextualized theological education requires a location in the midst of the people who are being served. The decision to purchase the building was affirmed by the students who had previously experienced the program and had a vested ownership in it. When the property was secured, the student body immediately identified with the location and referred to it as "our building." This ownership of the site was the fruit of the commitment of the previous fourteen years.

The importance of location is also demonstrated in CUME's decentralized classroom facilities. While there is the centralized administrative building, which houses offices, two conference rooms, and a library, courses are taught in several locations across the city.

Currently CUME uses four church or parachurch buildings for classroom instruction. In a sense, this is an adaptation of theological education by extension, whereby the courses are taken to the people. This Pilgrim Seminary model allows for greater flexibility in scheduling of courses; it lets us tailor specific courses for a particular community. More subtly, it also requires people from various ethnic groups to enter other communities to attend classes. Of course, this has resulted in some students staying away from CUME when they discovered that their course was to be offered in the African-American community or the Hispanic community, but such is life. Interestingly enough, the motivation to take a course often results in people overcoming their biases against a particular community and going to a particular site to take a course they want. Once there, the biases often begin to disappear.

Focus

The city is also the focus of CUME's ministry. Rather than seeing the city as inherently evil, CUME's philosophy is that it is the place where God redemptively is at work. Thus, the Shalom of the city is the commitment of both staff and students. A wholistic gospel that includes evangelism and social concern is encompassed. The incidents of gang violence in Boston in 1992 have elicited a response from the clergy to challenge the church to be more intentional in "hitting the streets." Many are CUME alumni/ae, students, faculty, or staff.

Leadership

Though the urban church has many gifted indigenous leaders, many urban programs are still supervised by white directors. This is not to say that whites should not be involved in urban theological educational programs, but the leadership should reflect the constituency that is served. Administratively, CUME does this. There is a diverse administrative staff, comprised of African Americans (2), Hispanics (3), and Anglos (2), reflecting the diversity of CUME's constituency. The fact that the staff live in the city means that they take an active interest in its welfare. All of the staff members are actively involved in churches and ministries that deal with the issues of urban life.

The administrative issue is not one of demographic representation. It goes to the heart of how things are run. This, of course, involves structures, policies, programs, and the like. By having an administration that is indigenous, there is a heightened sensitivity to doing things that outsiders might miss. What may appear to be a "good business" decision to one culture may be interpreted as uncaring or unfeeling in another. A case in point: At one point in CUME's history, we discussed the feasibility of sending out the grade reports along with the tuition bills. It was argued that this would cut down on mailing costs and staff time in preparing two separate mailings. One of the staff quietly suggested that this might offend students and communicate something that we did not really intend. As a result, the decision was made to send two separate mailings, and this decision has been codified as an official practice.

Ethics

Contextualization includes such intangible things as ethos and atmosphere. If students determine that their concerns are taken seriously, they will have ownership over the program. As part of Gordon-Conwell Theological Seminary, CUME must deal with the realities of a larger institution with its own peculiar bureaucracy. A similar situation exists in many larger churches or denominational structures. Bureaucracies tend to evolve into forms and patterns that meet their needs, but may or may not consider the individual needs of each student. People must conform to the rules of the game as defined by the bureaucracy.

CUME has made a conscious effort to reduce the burden of the bureaucracy on the student. This is not so much a factor of size, since CUME services almost 300 students per year (representing 150 distinct churches from 40 denominations and 22 nationalities), but is more of a commitment to keeping things as simple as possible. It also reflects our awareness of the fact that many urban people go through life at the mercy of the larger, impersonal institutions of the city.

CUME seeks to break with this traditional, impersonal model in an effort to affirm people's humanity, to communicate to them that they are valuable as people, not just a commodity or a product. An example of this is the manner in which students finance their tuition. Most schools require full payment at the beginning of the semester. CUME has provided for a "pay-as-you-go" policy that enables students to chip away at their bill a little bit at a time. CUME staff are required to be at the various class sites to receive payment, which means that they must work the evenings when classes are being taught. Though this can be demanding on the staff, there is a commitment to making theological education more accessible to our students.

Cost

The cost of the program should reflect the socioeconomic reality of the people who participate. One of the realities of the inner city is that its residents tend to be poorer financially (though rich in many other ways). Since many inner-city people are unable to afford the high costs of residential seminary education, a contextualized urban theological education program has costs that reflect this reality. Gordon-Conwell Theological Seminary has been committed to urban ministry, helping to underwrite the cost of CUME over its eighteen-year history. The low cost of tuition reflects a substantial built-in scholarship for students. As part of this commitment, a full-time director of annual giving was hired recently to assist the center in encouraging support from the constituent community and churches.

Language

The language of instruction should reflect the constituents. Since our cities are dynamic, one must wrestle with changing demographics and immigration patterns. When CUME began in 1976, there was a burgeoning growth of Hispanic churches in Boston. It was natural for CUME to begin as a fully bilingual program in English and Spanish. The fact that CUME's founding director, Dr. Eldin Villafañe, is Hispanic also played a strong role in this decision. In 1982, recognizing the growth of the Haitian and Portuguese-speaking communities, their two languages were added. In 1991, Theological Education for the Deaf began, with courses taught in American Sign Language.[3]

Each community may experience a rapid influx, but at some point the growth slows down and the assimilation process begins. The second and third generations of immigrant groups become more and more English-dominant. A contextualized theological program allows for this shift in language, all the while trying to maintain and encourage the use of one's native tongue — not in an attempt to ghettoize a person, but to enable them to relate to their native culture. The impact of being taught in one's native tongue, even though a person knows English, cannot be underestimated. That CUME teaches in five different languages is an affirmation of the essence of the people who speak them.

PRAXIS-FOCUSED MINISTRY

A praxis-based model of urban leadership training relates closely to the concept of contextualization. However, I would like to examine this aspect of a training program as a separate concept.

A distinction should be made between *praxis* and *practice*.[4] Practice of ministry is the doing of things as they relate to ministry. Things such as preaching, counseling, community organizing, and administration contain elements of ministerial practice or functioning. Praxis involves the doing of these skills, but it adds theological reflection upon what is being done, why it is done, how it is done, and what could be done. It marries action (doing) with reflection (being). The action must

---

3. Theological Education for the Deaf (T.E.D.) is a particular ministerial calling of Rev. Lorraine C. Anderson, coordinator of Student Advisement and Academic Services. The inclusion of T.E.D. as one of CUME's language tracks is recognition that the deaf comprise a unique cultural as well as linguistic community and require instruction fitted to meet that reality.

4. Much of my thinking on this issue stems from such sources as Paulo Freire, *Pedagogy of the Oppressed*, trans. Myra Bergman Ramos (New York: Continuum, 1981); F. Ross Kinsler, ed., *Ministry by the People: Theological Education by Extension* (Maryknoll, N.Y.: Orbis, 1983), and conversations with Dr. Eldin Villafañe, founding director of the Center for Urban Ministerial Education.

seek to transform the world,[5] and theological reflection must be done to understand and shape the acting process. The problem many of us face is that we often emphasize one at the expense of the other. A good training program for urban church leaders should foster both action and reflection. This is easier said than done, however.

At CUME, students are actively engaged in ministry while they are involved in classroom experiences. The material they learn is tested in their ministry, and the experiences of ministry become the substance for examination and reflection in the classroom. This is one of the major differences between CUME and residential seminary programs. Residential seminary training focuses, by and large, on "pre-service" training for ministry; CUME emphasizes "in-service" training. A criticism of residential seminaries is that they frequently apply answers to questions that students are not even asking. And worse than giving answers to questions that have not been asked yet is the tendency to tell students what the questions ought to be! Not only are students who are in ministry more motivated to find answers to their questions, they ask more questions of their situations than do those in a pre-service residential program. This is not to disparage the pre-service training aspects for urban ministry; this, too, is part of the overall ministry of CUME. It does, however, suggest that the best and most efficient way to learn how to do urban ministry is to do it while you are engaged in serious theological reflection on it. Action and reflection are joined as partners in a never-ending dialogue. Each informs the other.

One of the ways in which CUME has attempted to foster this action-reflection model is found in its Mentored Ministry Program[6] for degree students. Each student is paired with a mentor, who comes alongside as more of a guide than an expert. Both the mentor and the student are learners, walking for a time down the same path. The focus of the program is student-directed learning. A learning covenant is drawn up, based upon the student's goals and desired learning objectives. Weekly meetings with the mentor help the student to process the

5. See Gustavo Gutiérrez, *A Theology of Liberation* (Maryknoll, N.Y.: Orbis, 1971).

6. Much of the seminal thinking and design of this program has been done by Dr. Ira V. Frazier, assistant director for Church Relations and Mentored Ministry, who directs it. This information is drawn from conversations with him as well as from the CUME catalog.

events and "doings" of urban ministry. As the mentoring program unfolds, the student is encouraged to examine the foundations of his or her ministerial calling, identify gifts and areas of weakness, all in the context of the mentoring relationship.

Concurrent with the mentoring relationships are a series of four colloquia designed to probe and prod the students to continue in further reflection upon their experiences, the Word of God, and their own identity. The colloquia emphasize ministerial self-identity as well as assessing one's community and the relationship between the two. Students are encouraged to be wholistic in their ministerial approach, discovering how they function as ministers in society as well as in the church. The final component of this program involves the director of mentored ministry, who acts as a facilitator for each mentoring relationship, meeting regularly with each student and mentor, training mentors, and directing and teaching the four colloquia. The overall goal of mentored ministry is to help students understand their own unique place in the body of Christ and help them to see urban ministry as something for the long haul, something that requires cultivating the inner life as well as public presence.

By design, this focus on ministry and praxis requires a part-time model for structured theological education. CUME makes no apologies for designing its programs to appeal to the part-time student. Since many ministers in the urban setting are not full-time, paid staff in their churches, they often must work at a secular job for financial reasons. CUME's part-time focus allows them to study while working full-time and ministering in their church (often on a full-time basis). In a very real sense, students apply what they learned on Tuesday to the needs they encounter on Sunday morning. I recall a student who took the material on evangelizing the cults that he learned in a Wednesday night class and taught it in his adult Sunday school class the very next week. Talk about mastery learning — he was forcing himself to learn the material well enough to teach to others! And he was empowering his church for ministry at the same time.

This part-time orientation determines when the courses are taught. Our courses are offered in three basic time slots: late afternoons, evenings, and weekends. This makes it possible for a student to take two courses on one evening, keeping other evenings free for church or ministry obligations. This also allows students who commute from a distance to travel on only one night. CUME draws students from as far away as southern Maine, Rhode Island, northern Connecticut, and the western part of Massachusetts.

The content of the curriculum of an urban leadership training program should be focused on the practice of ministry. This is not to say that the theoretical aspects of ministry are ignored. They are not. But the philosophy of education that has guided CUME for the past eighteen years is the emphasis on doing ministry. Courses such as "Christian Social Action" involve a heavy concentration of social ethics (theory/theology) with a site placement involving the student in some activity related to the problems of society and its structures. In courses such as this, students learn aspects of "social analysis" that are critical to their own practice of theologizing in urban ministry.

Language courses such as Greek or Hebrew (a requirement of CUME's M.Div. in Urban Ministries degree) are taught in such a way that students see the importance of learning the original language to enhance their own understanding of Scripture, as well as to exegete the Word for more effective communication of the gospel. A course that I co-teach, "Research and Writing in Urban Theological Studies," focuses on the writing of academic papers related to theological education. Yet it also attempts to build on existing writing and research skills, to teach new ones, and to encourage students to view research and writing as a way to enhance their ministries. We tell them, "If you can write well and marshall your arguments effectively, you are in a better position to 'hustle' the system." Effective communication skills in a culture that values clear writing will give one access to resources previously unavailable to students and their churches. In a word, it provides empowerment.

GROUNDED IN THE PRESENT, LOOKING TO THE FUTURE

One of the most basic assumptions of any leadership training or educational program is that there is a future that awaits the church or ministry. Theologically, this hope is grounded in our anticipation of Christ's second advent. A program designed to train urban church leaders must convey this sense of hope even in times that seem to defy any reason for hope to exist. How is this to be done?

The first way is to affirm the cultural identities of the students — who they are, where they have come from, their present struggles, and their hopes and fears for the future. This, of course, relates to contextualization and to the praxis orientation described above. In a very real sense, the present reality can be understood only by examining the past, for in the past are links to the present struggle.[7] I do not need to detail the linkages between slavery and segregation and the racism that characterizes our national condition. They are clearly evident in events such as the 1992 riots in Los Angeles. What is instructive is how persons of color have managed to surmount this legacy with creativity, resourcefulness, grace, dignity, and, yes, even a sense of victory. This needs to be affirmed, not just for persons of color, but for the dominant Anglo culture as well.

One way this can be done is to expand the sources of information to include non-European authors and thinkers in addition to the so-called theological classics. There are heroes of the faith in every ethnic culture. They need to be identified and studied. It is preferable that these sources be written in the native tongue of the student, whether that be Spanish, Creole, Portuguese, or Vietnamese. Of course this means being creative in acquiring literature.[8] If written sources are difficult to locate, other nonwritten sources such as storytelling, recordings, and videos may provide information that affirms a person's culture and faith.

A second way to be grounded in the present, while looking to the future, involves the analytical tools and research base used. No program geared to training urban church leaders can afford to focus on the past, or even solely on the present. Research, no matter how formal or informal, must be done in order to plan for the future. Many programs, however, are so busy existing from day to day that future planning is done poorly, or not at all. Ongoing research that will benefit the program must be done.

Harvie Conn writes that such "research must be oriented to hope, not shame over past failures or guilt over missed opportunities . . . it

---

7. See, e.g., bell hooks, "Chitlin Circuit," *The Other Side*, March-April 1991, where she presents a cogent argument for knowing one's history as a way to continue onward in the journey.

8. The Center for Urban Ministerial Education is fortunate to be associated with the Fellowship-Emanuel Bookstore, which handles our textbook orders, drawing upon language books from sources in Canada and Latin America as well as in Europe.

must point to the obligation of service . . . [and it] must promote awe and reverence."[9] Research and study must emphasize an understanding of the present in light of the past, but it also must lead to action in transforming hope for the future. Again this relates to the process of doing social analysis, which informs one's theology and thus one's actions in ministry.

An urban leadership training program must build upon and expand on this theme of hope. Otherwise, one will be left with a pile of data that describes the situation but does not prescribe ways to improve it. It is fine to use demographic data to describe community conditions, but we must ask, does this help the student see the power of the gospel to transform what exists into what could be?

One aspect of research involves the use of models and telling "stories." One key way people learn about doing urban ministry is by hearing and observing others who are doing it. Sharing information about what others are doing is invaluable. This should permeate all levels of the training program, including administrators, faculty, and other leaders.

Modeling is also important for students. Through stories, case studies, site visits, and presentations about one's own ministry, a sense of hope can be communicated. Students are able to see themselves in aspects of the models and stories studied. There is something encouraging about hearing about others' past successes and failures. As fellow students share about what has happened to them, you can almost see the lightbulb go on in another person's head when he or she realizes, "Hey, I've experienced that before, that's happened to me. Maybe there is light at the end of the tunnel." By sharing their stories, students encourage one another to hang on in a tough situation.

Douglas Hall, director of the Emmanuel Gospel Center and one of CUME's professors, stresses the need for urban practitioners to analyze models as completely as possible in order to learn from their mistakes and successes. He stresses experimenting as much as possible on paper before you experiment on people. While this may seem to be an obvious truth, my experience has been that it is not done or not done well. CUME strives to reflect this attitude in the way it designs

9. Harvie Conn, "Micro Reminders for Macro Researchers," in *SCUPE Urban Researchers and Resource Centers Directory* (Chicago: SCUPE, 1992), pp. 6-8.

new programs. Models of other programs are analyzed before anything is launched. This way, potential problems are anticipated and hopefully minimized.

SERVANT LEADERSHIP

The fourth major characteristic that is necessary for an urban leadership training program can be termed "servant leadership." Again, this can take many forms, but I would like to suggest four ways that this can be fleshed out programmatically.

Servant leadership involves partnership with the existing indigenous church leadership. By this I mean that the program must be seen by these leaders as complementing their ministries, not competing with them. A servant orientation approaches existing leaders with respect and asks, "How could we serve you and the needs of your people?" instead of "Here is a great program that will really meet all of your needs." If one ignores the gatekeepers to various communities, the likelihood that these leaders will send students to a training program will be greatly reduced.

A desire to serve the churches is laced throughout CUME's history. In fact, CUME only offered courses in new languages after months of dialogue with community leaders. In effect CUME said to these leaders, "You push us. We'll establish something that you want, but you must push us. We'll move as fast as you want us to move." This is not to suggest that one must be co-opted by dominant or domineering leaders. It does suggest, however, that serving the churches means empowering the existing leadership at the same time that you train the newer leaders who are being raised up.

An emphasis on servant leadership also affects the way courses are structured to accommodate clergy and laity. At CUME, we do not separate courses for clergy and laity. They can be found in the same classroom, taking the same courses. This, of course, may threaten the clergy when they realize that a church member may actually be a better student than they are. The experience, however, has been almost uniformly positive. Since all students are seen as "ministers," the clergy-laity barriers have begun to evaporate. Clergy have a new respect for the laity;

and laity begin to realize their part in the overall ministry of the church. There have been cases where clergy have refused to participate in our courses, but this seems to have faded in most constituencies. What is emphasized is the need for the whole people of God to be about the whole task of God.

A servant-oriented leadership training program focuses on Christianity in the entire city, not just on one's particular ministry. It looks to see how development of my particular ministry affects those around me. This fosters an atmosphere of cooperation rather than competition, of celebration when someone else succeeds, of caring when someone else is hurting. While this is certainly taught in the classroom, it is more effectively modeled by the way CUME operates. CUME views itself in partnership with existing churches and ministries for the sake of seeing the expansion of Christianity in Boston. While we know our particular role, we also hold strong convictions that our ministry is a shared one. This has resulted in exceptionally supportive relationships with the Emmanuel Gospel Center and Twelfth Baptist Church as our ministry has developed and grown.

The mutual respect that CUME has for its constituent churches is also seen in its style of leadership. Begun under Dr. Eldin Villafañe and continuing under Dr. Efraín Agosto, the style of leadership at CUME is truly collegial. It is my conviction that how a program is structured and operates reveals whether or not it believes in servant leadership. Though there is a defined chain of responsibility, the operational ethos of CUME is one of trust and respect. A hierarchical, top-down style does not prevail in the administration. To a certain degree, this is due to the size of the staff and to the fact that each staff member does a variety of tasks and can, when needed, "pinch-hit" for someone else. Staff members genuinely like and support one another, to the extent that we refer to ourselves as the "CUME family." My colleagues are some of the most creative and gifted people I know. It is simply a joy to work with each of them. This joy, this sense of serving one another, rubs off on how CUME deals with its students.

Conclusion

What makes for a good urban ministry training program? The concept of contextualization suggests that it must fit the situation in which it is located. This, of course, means that it will be necessary to adapt some of the elements I have highlighted from CUME to fit the particular context. The concept of praxis — of a program that combines ministry practice with theological reflection — is the second element, whether a structured or informal program is envisioned. Third, there must be a sense of hope that knows the past and its impact on the present, but looks toward the future. This involves affirmation, research, and modeling. Finally, the fourth concept is servant leadership. Empowering the existing leadership while training newer leadership is essential. Empowering the whole church to minister to the larger city must be modeled by the training program, in both its external and internal relationships.

I have drawn heavily on my experiences at the Center for Urban Ministerial Education. This was done intentionally, but not uncritically. CUME is far from the perfect program. However, it has stood the test of time and done so with integrity. It provides a model for others to examine, critique, emulate, or reject. It is in this spirit that this article was written.

Bibliography

Albizu Campos, Pedro. *La Conciencia Nacional Puertorriqueña.* Mexico, D.F.: Siglo Veintiuno, 1974.

Allen, Roland. *Missionary Methods: St. Paul's or Ours?* Reprint, Grand Rapids: Eerdmans, 1962.

Alves, Ruben. *Protestantism and Repression.* Maryknoll, N.Y.: Orbis Books, 1985.

Arana Quiroz, Pedro. "Ordenes de la Creación y Responsabilidad Cristiana." In C. René Padilla, ed., *Fe Cristiana y Latinoamerica Hoy.* Buenos Aires: Ediciones Certeza, 1974.

Arias, Mortimer. *Salvación es Liberación.* Buenos Aires: La Aurora, 1973.

Augustine. *Confessions* 2. New York: Random House, 1949.

Bakke, Raymond. *The Urban Christian: Effective Ministry in Today's Urban World.* Downers Grove, Ill.: InterVarsity Press, 1987.

Barton, S. "Paul and the Cross: A Sociological Approach." *Theology* 85, no. 73 (1982).

Bellah, Robert. "Evil and the American Ethos." In *Sanctions for Evil,* ed. Nevitt Sandord and Craig Comstock. San Francisco: Jossey-Bass, 1971.

Berger, Peter L. *The Sacred Canopy: Elements of a Sociological Theory of Religion.* New York: Anchor Books, 1969.

Berger, Peter L., and Thomas Luckman. *The Social Construction of Reality: A Treatise in the Sociology of Knowledge.* New York: Anchor Books, 1967.

Berkhof, Hendrikus. *Christ and the Powers.* Scottdale, Pa.: Herald Press, 1962.

Betsworth, Roger G. *Social Ethics: An Examination of American Moral Traditions.* Louisville, Ky.: Westminster/John Knox Press, 1990.

Bloesch, Donald G. *The Struggle of Prayer.* Colorado Springs, Col.: Helmers & Howard, 1988.

Bright, John. *The Kingdom of God.* Nashville: Abingdon Press, 1953.

Browning, Don S. *A Fundamental Practical Theology.* Minneapolis: Fortress Press, 1991.

Brunner, Emil. *The Divine Imperative.* Philadelphia: Westminster Press, 1937.

"Census Says Good Life Still Eludes Most of US Hispanic Population." *The Boston Globe,* April 11, 1991.

Cisneros, Henry G., ed. *Interwoven Destinies: Cities and the Nation.* New York: W. W. Norton & Company, 1993.

Conn, Harvie. *A Clarified Vison for Urban Mission: Dispelling the Urban Stereotypes.* Grand Rapids: Zondervan Publishing House, 1987.

————. "Micro Reminders for Macro Researchers." In *SCUPE Urban Researchers and Resource Centers Directory.* Chicago: SCUPE, 1992.

Costas, Orlando. *Christ Outside the Gate: Mission Beyond Christendom.* Maryknoll, N.Y.: Orbis Books, 1982.

————. "Hispanic Theology in North America." B.T.I., Liberation Theology Consultation, Andover Newton Theological School, October 25, 1986.

————. *The Integrity of Mission: The Inner Life and Outreach of the Church.* New York: Harper and Row, 1979.

————. "Social Justice in the Other Protestant Tradition: A Hispanic Perspective." In *Contemporary Ethical Issues in the Jewish and Christian Traditions,* ed. Frederick Greenspahn. Hoboken, N.J.: Ktau Publishing House, 1986.

Cox, Harvey. *Religion in the Secular City: Toward a Postmodern Theology.* New York: Simon and Schuster, 1984.

Delgado, Melvin, and Denise Humn-Delgado. "Natural Support Systems: Source of Strength in Hispanic Communities." *Social Work,* January 1982.

Dezell, Maureen. "The Third Coming." *The Boston Phoenix,* June 22-28, 1990.

Elizondo, Virgilio. *Galilean Journey: The Mexican-American Promise.* Maryknoll, N.Y.: Orbis Books, 1983.

Ellis, E. Earle. "Paul and His Co-Workers." *New Testament Studies* 17 (1971).

Ellul, Jacques. *The Subversion of Christianity.* Grand Rapids: Eerdmans, 1987.

Farley, Edward. *Theologia.* Philadelphia: Fortress Press, 1983.

Flanagan, William G. *Contemporary Urban Sociology.* New York: Cambridge University Press, 1993.

Forrester, Jay W. *Urban Dynamics.* Cambridge, Mass.: The M.I.T. Press, 1969.

Freire, Paulo. *The Pedagogy of the Oppressed.* New York: Seabury Press, 1970.

Fukuyama, Francis. "The Power of the Powerless." In *The End of History and the Last Man.* New York: The Free Press, 1992.

Glazer, Nathan, and Patrick Moynihan. *Beyond the Melting Pot.* Cambridge, Mass.: The M.I.T. Press, 1963.

González, Justo. *Faith and Wealth: A History of Early Christian Ideas on the Origin, Significance, and Use of Money.* San Francisco: Harper and Row, 1990.

————. *The Hispanic Ministry of the Episcopal Church in the Metropolitan Area of New York and Environs.* New York: Grants Program of Trinity Parish, 1985.

————. *Mañana: Christian Theology from a Hispanic Perspective.* Nashville: Abingdon Press, 1990.

————. *The Theological Education of Hispanics.* New York: The Fund for Theological Education, 1988.

Gordon, Milton M. *Assimilation in American Life: The Role of Race, Religion and National Origins.* New York: Oxford University Press, 1964.

Greenway, Roger S. *Apostles to the City: Biblical Strategies for Urban Missions.* Grand Rapids: Baker Book House, 1978.

————, ed. *Discipling the City: A Comprehensive Approach to Urban Mission.* Grand Rapids: Baker Book House, 1992.

Gutiérrez, Gustavo. *The Power of the Poor in History.* Maryknoll, N.Y.: Orbis Books, 1983.

————. *A Theology of Liberation.* Maryknoll, N.Y.: Orbis Books, 1971.

————. *We Drink from Our Own Wells: The Spiritual Journey of a People.* Maryknoll, N.Y.: Orbis Books, 1984.

Harrington, Daniel. "Second Testament Exegesis and the Social Sciences: A Bibliography." *Biblical Theology Bulletin* 18 (1988).

Havel, Václav. "The Power of the Powerless." In *Open Letters: Selected Writings, 1965–1990.* New York: Alfred A. Knopf, 1991.

Hock, Ronald. *The Social Context of Paul's Ministry: Tentmaking and Apostleship.* Philadelphia: Fortress Press, 1980.

Holmberg, Bengt. *Paul and Power: The Structure of Authority in the Primitive*

Church as Reflected in the Pauline Epistles. Philadelphia: Fortress Press, 1978.

hooks, bell. "Chitlin Circuit." *The Other Side,* March-April 1991.

Hopler, Thom. *A World of Difference: Following Christ Beyond Your Cultural Walls.* Downers Grove, Ill.: InterVarsity Press, 1981.

Isasi-Diaz, Ada Maria. *En la Lucha/In the Struggle: A Hispanic Women's Liberation Theology.* Minneapolis: Fortress Press, 1993.

Jackson, Bruce. "The Center for Urban Ministerial Education (CUME): Impact on Boston." Unpublished report, Boston, Mass., 1990.

Kelsey, Morton. *Discernment: A Study in Ecstasy and Evil.* New York: Paulist Press, 1978.

Kerans, Patrick. *Sinful Social Structures.* New York: Paulist Press, 1974.

King, Martin Luther, Jr. *Strength to Love.* London: Wm. Collins and Sons, 1963.

King, Mel. *Chain of Changes: Struggles for Black Community Development.* Boston, Mass.: South End Press, 1981.

Kinsler, F. Ross, ed. *Ministry by the People: Theological Education by Extension.* Maryknoll, N.Y.: Orbis Books, 1983.

Kittel, Gerhard, ed. *Theological Dictionary of the New Testament,* trans. Geoffrey W. Bromiley. Grand Rapids: Eerdmans, 1964.

Ladd, George Eldon. *The Presence of the Future: The Eschatology of Biblical Realism.* Grand Rapids: Eerdmans, 1974.

———. *A Theology of the New Testament.* Grand Rapids: Eerdmans, 1983.

Lane, George A. *Christian Spirituality: An Historical Sketch.* Chicago: Loyola University Press, 1984.

Linthicum, Robert C. *City of God City of Satan: A Biblical Theology of the Urban Church.* Grand Rapids: Zondervan Publishing House, 1991.

———. *Empowering the Poor: Community Organizing Among the City's "Rag, Tag and Bobtail."* Monrovia, Calif.: MARC, 1991.

Lovelace, Richard. *Dynamics of Spiritual Life: An Evangelical Theology of Renewal.* Downers Grove, Ill.: InterVarsity Press, 1979.

MacMullen, Ramsey. *Roman Social Relations: 50 B.C. to A.D. 284.* New Haven: Yale University Press, 1974.

Meehan, Frances X. *A Contemporary Social Spirituality.* Maryknoll, N.Y.: Orbis Books, 1982.

Meeks, Wayne. *The First Urban Christians.* New Haven: Yale University Press, 1983.

Mitchell, Rudy, and Eldin Villafañe. "The Center for Urban Ministerial

Education: A Case Study in Theological Education by Extension." *New England Journal of Ministry* 1, no. 2 (March 1981).

Moltmann, Jürgen. *The Crucified God: The Cross of Christ as the Foundation and Criticism of Christian Theology.* New York: Harper and Row, 1974.

Moore, Joan, and Raguel Pinderhughes. *In the Barrios: Latinos and the Underclass Debate.* New York: Russell Sage Foundation, 1993.

Mott, Stephen C. *Biblical Ethics and Social Change.* New York: Oxford University Press, 1982.

Nash, Joe. "Multiethnic Ministries." *Black Guard,* Black Christian Education Resources Center, Winter 1978.

"New Alternatives for Theological Education." *Fraternidad Teologica Latinoamericana.* Quito, 1985, mimeographed.

Novak, Michael. *The Rise of the Unmeltable Ethnics: Politics and Culture in the Seventies.* New York: Macmillan, 1971.

Ortiz, Manuel. *The Hispanic Challenge: Opportunities Confronting the Church.* Downers Grove, Ill.: InterVarsity Press, 1993.

Padilla, C. René. *Misión Integral: Ensayos Sobre el Reino y la Iglesia.* Grand Rapids: Eerdmans, 1986.

———. *Nuevas Alternativas de Educacion Teologica.* Grand Rapids: Eerdmans, 1986.

Palen, John J. *The Urban World.* 3rd ed. New York: McGraw-Hill Book Company, 1987.

Paz, Octavio. "Reflections." *The New Yorker,* November 17, 1979. In Ruben P. Armendariz, "Hispanic Heritage and Christian Education." *ALERT,* November 1981.

Pazmiño, Robert. *Foundational Issues in Christian Education: An Introduction in Evangelical Perspective.* Grand Rapids: Baker Book House, 1988.

———. *The Seminary in the City: A Study of New York Theological Seminary.* Lanham: University Press of America, 1988.

Prud'Homme, Alex. "Race Relations: Brown vs. Black." *TIME,* July 29, 1993.

"Purpose Sub-Committee Report: Theological Education in and for an Urban Global Village." Unpublished report in The Center for Urban Ministerial Education: Evaluation and Long Range Planning Project, Boston, Mass., 1987.

Rauschenbusch, Walter. *A Theology for the Social Gospel.* New York: Macmillan, 1917.

Recinos, Harold J. *Jesus Weeps: Global Encounter on Our Doorstep.* Nashville: Abingdon Press, 1992.

Ridderbos, Herman. *The Coming of the Kingdom.* Philadelphia: Presbyterian and Reformed, 1962.

Robinson, H. Wheeler. *Corporate Personality in Ancient Israel.* Philadelphia: Fortress Press, 1964.

Rodriguez, Clara. "Puerto Rican: Between Black and White." In *The Puerto Rican Struggle,* ed. Clara Rodriguez et al. New York: Puerto Rican Migration Research Consortium, 1980.

Rotenberg, Robert, and Gary McDonough, eds. *The Cultural Meaning of Urban Space.* Westport, Conn.: Bergin & Garvey, 1993.

Rowland, C., and M. Corner. *Liberating Exegesis: The Challenge of Liberation Theology to Biblical Studies.* Philadelphia: Westminster Press, 1989.

Sampley, J. Paul. *Pauline Partnership in Christ: Christian Community and Commitment in Light of Roman Law.* Philadelphia: Fortress Press, 1980.

Sanchez, David. "Viable Models for Churches in Communities Experiencing Ethnic Transition." Paper, Fuller Theological Seminary, 1976. In C. Peter Wagner, *Our Kind of People: The Ethical Dimensions of Church Growth in America.* Atlanta: John Knox Press, 1979.

Schön, Donald. *The Reflective Practitioner: How Professionals Think in Action.* New York: Basic Books, 1983.

Schwab, William A. *The Sociology of Cities.* Englewood Cliffs, N.J.: Prentice-Hall, 1992.

Scott Meyers, Eleanor, ed. *Envisioning the New City: A Reader on Urban Ministry.* Louisville, Ky.: Westminster/John Knox Press, 1992.

Shorris, Earl. *Latinos: A Biography of the People.* New York: Avon Books, 1992.

Shutz, John. *Paul and the Anatomy of Apostolic Authority.* Cambridge: Cambridge University Press, 1975.

Stackhouse, Max L. *Apologia: Contextualization, Globalization, and Mission in Theological Education.* Grand Rapids: Eerdmans, 1988.

Stone, Clarence N., Robert K. Whelan, and William J. Murin. *Urban Policy and Politics in a Bureaucratic Age.* 2nd ed. Englewood Cliffs, N.J.: Prentice-Hall, 1986.

Stronstad, Roger. *The Charismatic Theology of St. Luke.* Peabody, Mass.: Hendrikson Publishers, 1984.

Theissen, Gerd. "Social Stratification in the Corinthian Community." In *The Social Setting of Pauline Christianity: Essays on Corinth.* Philadelphia: Fortress Press, 1982.

Thomas, Piri. *Savior, Savior, Hold My Hand.* Garden City, N.Y.: Doubleday and Co., 1972.

Tidball, Derek. *The Social Context of the New Testament: A Sociological Analysis.* Grand Rapids: Zondervan, 1984.

Villafañe, Eldin. *The Liberating Spirit: Toward an Hispanic American Pentecostal Social Ethic.* Grand Rapids: Eerdmans, 1993.

Vobejda, Barbara. "Broad Growth Is Found in U.S. Hispanic, Asian Population." *The Boston Globe,* March 11, 1991.

Walker, Theodore, Jr. *Empower the People: Social Ethics for the African-American Church.* Maryknoll, N.Y.: Orbis Books, 1991.

Wallis, Jim. *Agenda for a Biblical People.* New York: Harper and Row, 1976.

Webber, George. *Led by the Spirit: The Story of New York Theological Seminary.* New York: The Pilgrim Press, 1990.

————, and Helen Webber. *The Center for Urban Ministerial Education — An Evaluation 1986-87: Contextualized Urban Theological Education.* Boston, Mass.: Gordon-Conwell Theological Seminary, 1987.

Wells, David F. *God the Evangelist: How the Holy Spirit Works to Bring Men and Women to Faith.* Grand Rapids: Eerdmans, 1987.

West, Cornel. *Race Matters.* Boston: Beacon Press, 1993.

Wilder, Amos N. "Kerygma, Eschatology and Social Ethics." In *The Background of the New Testament and Its Eschatology,* ed. W. D. Davies and D. Daube. Cambridge: Cambridge University Press, 1956.

Wimber, John. *Power Evangelism.* San Francisco: Harper and Row, 1986.

Wink, Walter. *Naming the Powers: The Language of Powers in the New Testament.* Philadelphia: Fortress Press, 1984.

————. *Unmasking the Powers: The Invisible Forces that Determine Human Existence.* Philadelphia: Fortress Press, 1986.

Yoder, John H. *The Politics of Jesus.* Grand Rapids: Eerdmans, 1972.

Contributors

Efraín Agosto is dean of Gordon-Conwell Theological Seminary's Center for Urban Ministerial Education (CUME) in Boston. Dr. Agosto is an educator, pastor, and New Testament scholar. He earned his Ph.D. in New Testament and Christian Origins from Boston University.

Harvey Cox is Victor S. Thomas Professor of Divinity at the Harvard Divinity School. Dr. Cox is the author of *The Secular City, Feast of Fools, Many Mansions, The Silencing of Leonardo Boff, Religion in the Secular City,* and, most recently, *Fire from Heaven,* among other works.

Douglas Hall has been the executive director of Emmanuel Gospel Center in Boston for over twenty-five years. He is an adjunct professor in urban studies at Gordon-Conwell Theological Seminary's Center for Urban Ministerial Education. Dr. Hall specializes in the area of urban ministry with particular interest in church planting, urban systems, and the effects short-term efforts have on the health of the church in the long term.

Bruce W. Jackson is program director, Contextualized Urban Theological Education Enablement Program (CUTEEP) of the Center for Urban Ministerial Education (CUME) in Boston. He has also served as associate director of CUME. Dr. Jackson is an urban theological educator whose expertise lies in the area of research, educational administration, and long-range planning. He earned his Ed.D. in Administration, Training, and Policy Studies from Boston University.

Eldin Villafañe is Professor of Christian Social Ethics at Gordon-Conwell Theological Seminary. He is the executive director of Contextualized Urban Theological Education Enablement Program (CUTEEP) of the Center for Urban Ministerial Education (CUME) in Boston. Dr. Villafañe was the founding director (1976–1990) of CUME and former associate dean of Urban and Multicultural Affairs at Gordon-Conwell Theological Seminary. He served as the first president of La Comunidad of Hispanic American Scholars of Theology and Religion, and currently is president of the Society for Pentecostal Studies (SPS). He earned his Ph.D. in Social Ethics from Boston University. Dr. Villafañe was recently named one of the nation's ten most influential Hispanic religious leaders and scholars by the *National Catholic Reporter*. He is the author of the highly acclaimed *The Liberating Spirit: Toward an Hispanic American Pentecostal Social Ethic*.